Pacific Coasting

Pacific Coasting

A Guide to
THE ULTIMATE ROAD TRIP,
from Southern California to
the Pacific Northwest

Danielle Kroll

Artisan | New York

Title page illustration: La Jolla Shores Beach

Library of Congress Cataloging-in-Publication Data

Names: Kroll, Danielle, author.
Title: Pacific coasting / Danielle Kroll.
Description: New York : Artisan, a division of Workman Publishing Co., Inc., 2020.
Identifiers: LCCN 2019048610 | ISBN 9781579658717 (hardcover)
Subjects: LCSH: Pacific Coast (U.S.)—Description and travel. | Pacific Coast (U.S.)—Guidebooks. | Pacific Coast Highway (Calif.–Wash.)—Guidebooks. | Automobile travel—Pacific Coast (U.S.)
Classification: LCC F851 .K76 2020 | DDC 979—dc23
LC record available at https://lccn.loc.gov/2019048610

Cover design and illustration by Danielle Kroll
Design by Raphael Geroni

Artisan books are available at special discounts when purchased in bulk for premiums and sales promotions as well as for fund-raising or educational use. Special editions or book excerpts also can be created to specification. For details, contact the Special Sales Director at the address below, or send an e-mail to specialmarkets@workman.com.

For speaking engagements, contact speakersbureau@workman.com.

Published by Artisan
A division of Workman Publishing Co., Inc.
225 Varick Street
New York, NY 10014-4381
artisanbooks.com

Artisan is a registered trademark of Workman Publishing Co., Inc.

Published simultaneously in Canada by Thomas Allen & Son, Limited

Printed in China

10 9 8 7 6 5 4 3 2

Contents

INTRODUCTION

Let me paint you a picture: You're in the car with your best friend/partner/ mom/sibling/children/own self. Music wafts from the speakers, the windows are down, and a brisk breeze tousles your hair. On your left is the expansive Pacific coastline, waves crashing on the beaches below. On your right, a forested cliffside, the trees stretched tall as if seeking out the best ocean view. As you wind up the coast, there's the promise of the open road, where experiencing the journey is as much the goal as your destination.

I grew up on the East Coast—in New Jersey, to be precise. I've always been inspired by the natural world, but on this side of the country, it's hard to avoid cities, where there are often more buildings than trees, more streets than rivers.

The Pacific coastline is different. Everything feels bigger, wilder, lusher. The landscape is something to coexist with, to be inspired by, instead of something to conquer. It calls out to be explored. Certainly there are towns and cities, strip malls and drive-throughs out west, but despite the urbanization, there is still a taste of the rugged environment that once was. This is why the Pacific coastline is so special to me. I feel energized and entranced by its thriving natural world.

Road trips are in my blood. When I was growing up, they were my family's preferred way of vacationing. My dad has always said that if he didn't have a family, he would have been a truck driver, simply because he loves driving that much. I inherited a touch of that from him. I do like the feeling of being behind the wheel, but what I love most about road trips is looking out the car window, listening to music, letting my thoughts wander, trying to take in everything as it passes by.

The Pacific coast offers uninterrupted time and space to do exactly that. Driving the Pacific Coast Highway is less stressful than freeway driving, and certainly more beautiful. And you can't really get lost. For most of the drive, you're on Highway 101, but to follow the route, you just hug the coastline, always going in the same direction. In driving the entirety of the 1,650 miles myself, I found that my few moments of panic came mostly from navigating through cities like Los Angeles and San Francisco and trying to find a parking spot in a full lot or on a busy street.

But while we romanticize the idea of road trips, they are a lot of work. You're constantly on the move, driving several hours at a time, unpacking and repacking. If you're craving a vacation where you lie around and do nothing for a week, this isn't it. But if you're looking to challenge yourself, to go on an adventure, to see something new every hour and every day, then take the long, winding road.

Whatever your travel spirit or your motivation, I am convinced that a road trip along the Pacific coast, or even along just a section, is a perfect vacation. Older adventurers hit the road in their RVs, young couples sleep in their camper vans on hidden dirt roads, and families pack into minivans destined for sunny days at the beach. It is a journey that can be shared or taken in solitude. I have done portions of this trip with my girlfriends, with my whole family, with just my mom, with my partner, alone . . . every trip along this coastline has inevitably led to the same result: a memorable vacation that left me feeling inspired and grateful.

A Short History of the Pacific Coastline

Native American people were the first to call this coastline home, thriving on the bounty offered by the forests and the seas, living in balanced harmony with the world around them. The first permanent European settlement on the Pacific coast dates to 1769, when Spanish colonial interests brought expeditioners to what is now San Diego, California. In the 1800s, commercial logging and fishing began to boom, building up small outposts into regional hubs for these new industries. Later, they would be forced to reckon with regulations and protections that would keep humans from entirely destroying all the natural bounty that made this region flourish.

In the 1930s, the coastal road that we now know as the Pacific Coast Highway was largely finished, making for an uninterrupted stretch along the western US coastline, introducing tourism to places that were otherwise difficult to reach. This helped open up the region to the rest of the world, and now towns up and down the coast have become premier tourist destinations, luring visitors to their historic downtowns with preserved estates, museums, aquariums, botanical gardens, restaurants, and antiques shops.

How to Use This Book

This book features some of my favorite spots along the coast, peppered with tidbits on local history and culture, as well as glimpses of the wild flora and fauna. But the places I mention certainly aren't the only ones worth stopping at: Consider the book a jumping-off point, an invitation for you to go out and explore.

While many people start in the north and work their way south, I always drive from south to north, so that is how the book flows. In this direction, there's another lane to buffer you from the cliff edge, which is helpful if heights make you uncomfortable, and the views get progressively more gorgeous and dramatic the farther north you go. However, the big allure of driving in the opposite direction, from north to south, is the unobstructed view of the ocean to your right, and the roadside lookouts are more convenient to pull into on a whim.

Given my interest in the natural world, when there is a rugged option, I will usually take it. I camp as often as I can, exploring steep, slippery hiking trails to get to the best tide pools. But this trip can be modified to suit your preferences and temperament. You'll find bed-and-breakfasts, charming hotels, and rental homes all along the route. There are plenty of opportunities to pad in rest days and pampered nights.

If you want to take a slower pace and not drive to a different location each day, or you don't have the luxury of time, pick a section of the coast and plan your vacation as a round-trip. Also note that travel time will vary depending on traffic.

When planning your itinerary, make a note of where you'd like to sleep each night. This will help to keep you on track, which is especially important in peak season (see page 17), when you need to book accommodations in advance. Include your "can't miss" spots on the itinerary, but leave room for serendipity too. Keep your eyes open at museums, visitor centers, and coffee shops for local events, and at hotels for brochures touting activities and places that interest you. Ask guides and locals what they recommend.

ENJOYING THE RIDE

- **GIVE YOURSELF ENOUGH TIME.** Plan to drive no more than four hours a day. Two hours is preferable, so you can get to a new destination and make impulse stops as well as those you've planned.

- **DON'T DRIVE TOO LONG AT NIGHT.** The gorgeous view of the ocean and forests is a central feature of this road trip. As well as keeping you from enjoying the landscape, driving after dark is more challenging because the roads aren't lit. A lot of the coastal rental homes are off the beaten path and can be tricky to find. Aim to arrive at your destination by nightfall.

- **DON'T TAILGATE!** For some stretches of this route, passing is permitted, but the majority is a two-lane highway with a double yellow line. Chill out, slow down, and enjoy the tranquil view around you. If someone tailgates you and you feel pressure to go faster, pull over at the next safe spot and let them pass. You'll both be thankful you did.

- **GAS UP.** Try not to let your gas gauge go below a quarter tank. There are very desolate areas on the coast, especially in Big Sur, California, and Washington State, where you may not see a gas station for hours and there's no cell service to look up where the next one is. (Note that in Oregon, gas stations are full-service.)

- **TAKE BREAKS.** Get out of the car whenever you make a stop. If your fellow passengers need a bathroom break and you don't, just stretch your legs.

- **TAKE TURNS.** If you're renting a car, make sure to have two registered drivers. Switch off driving duties so you don't get fatigued and everyone gets to enjoy the view. A good copilot doesn't just relax and nap. It's their job to keep the music flowing, to be on phone duty, and to navigate.

- **PLAN YOUR ROUTE.** Carry a printed map and download the data for the area you will be traveling through, which you can do in the morning before heading out for the day. Cell service and LTE are spotty along the coast, particularly in Northern California and the Pacific Northwest. If you have the area's map downloaded, you won't need service to navigate. To find the fastest route, GPS navigation will sometimes take you off the coastal road. For the optimal scenic route, ignore the navigation and continue along the coastal highway.

- **PARK AND WALK.** In popular areas, park away from the congestion and walk in. This will save you from hunting for a spot in traffic, and it may save you money too. When there is no choice but to park in a packed lot, be patient—trust in the welcoming spirit of the West Coast and a spot will open up eventually.

CAR PACKING LIST

Some things to pack or pick up on the way.

DUFFEL BAG. Instead of a suitcase, opt for a duffel bag, which you can easily unzip and rummage through while it's still in the trunk.

FIRST AID KIT. If it's old, make sure it's restocked.

HAND SANITIZER. For when soap isn't available at rest stops and campgrounds.

PAPER TOWELS. For inevitable spills.

PHONE ACCESSORIES. It's always good to bring your own car charger just in case the rental vehicle doesn't have one. And a phone mount is very useful if you plan on regularly using GPS for directions.

AUDIO CABLE. Make sure to download your playlists and podcasts onto your phone before you go so you can listen to them even when there's no cell service.

WATER JUG. Trailheads and beaches don't always have water spigots, so keep one or two jugs on hand in the car to ensure steady access to potable water.

REUSABLE WATER BOTTLE. Ditch disposable water bottles and fill up at rest stops, gas stations, restaurants, and public water fountains.

COOLER. Refill with ice from a grocery store or gas station.

SNACKS. Stock up on snacks that will make you feel good and keep you energized.

ALUMINUM FOIL. Wrap leftover food in it, form it into an incense holder, or use it as a plate.

PEPPERMINTS. Peppermint increases alertness and reduces stress.

PERSONAL PACKING LIST

CAMP PACKING LIST

Essentials to remember if you're camping.

TENT. A two-person backpacking tent is ideal for compact traveling.

SLEEPING BAG. A modern sleeping bag that can pack down small and accommodate 40-degree temperatures.

SLEEPING PAD. A foldable or blow-up that will pack up easily.

CAMP STOVE. Opt for a small stove that screws directly on to a fuel canister. Note that you can't bring a fuel canister on the airplane, so you'll need to buy one after you land.

POT, PAN, AND KETTLE. One pan for food and a pot or kettle to boil water for tea. To save room, buy a cheap pan from a thrift shop at the beginning of your trip and donate it at the end.

SILVERWARE, MUGS, AND A SMALL KNIFE FOR PREPARING FOOD.

HEADLAMP. Works way better than your cell phone light.

SMALL LANTERN, CANDLES, AND INCENSE. For light and to set the mood after the sun goes down. Incense keeps the bugs at bay.

A LIGHTER, MATCHES, AND NEWSPAPERS. Gather free newspapers along the way to use as kindling. You can buy firewood at your campsite.

SMALL PILLOW. Or roll up a comfy sweater.

CAMP SHOES. Comfortable slip-ons or sandals that you can wear with socks around the campground.

OPTIONAL. Face wipes or wet wipes, a sponge, a small bottle of dish soap, plates and bowls (or be creative with tin foil), a thermos, and a wool blanket.

ROAD TRIP PLAYLIST

Some songs to enjoy on the road!

"Ride Away"—Roy Orbison

"I Drove All Night"—Cyndi Lauper

"Feel Flows"—The Beach Boys

"California Dreamin' "
—The Mamas and the Papas

"Hitchin' a Ride"—Vanity Fare

"Come to the Sunshine"
—Harpers Bizarre

"Everybody's Talkin' "—Harry Nilsson

"The Big Sky"—Kate Bush

"Sea of Love"
—Phil Phillips & The Twilights

"On the Other Side"—The Seekers

"Pacific Ocean Blues"—Dennis Wilson

"Sloop John B"—The Beach Boys

"Summer Wine"
—Nancy Sinatra, Lee Hazlewood

"Going Up the Country"
—Canned Heat

"Rocky Road"—Peter, Paul and Mary

"Automechanic"—Jenny O.

"Catch a Wave"—The Beach Boys

"Optimistic Voices"
—from *The Wizard of Oz*

"Seabird"—Alessi Brothers

"On the Road Again"—Willie Nelson

"Wildflowers"
—Dolly Parton, Linda Ronstadt,
and Emmylou Harris

"Sacred Sands"—Allah-Las

"Everyday Is a Winding Road"
—Sheryl Crow

"Driving"—Everything but the Girl

"Pipeline"—The Ventures

"Magical Mystery Tour"—The Beatles

"Drive"—The Cars

"(Ghost) Riders in the Sky"
—Johnny Cash

"In the Pines"—Widowspeak

"Until We Get There"—Lucius

"Here I Go Again"—Whitesnake

"Running on Empty"
—Jackson Browne

"Road to Nowhere"—Talking Heads

"Beyond the Blue Horizon"
—Lou Christie

"End of the Line"
—Traveling Wilburys

WHEN TO GO

There is no perfect time to visit the Pacific coast; all seasons have their distinct moments that make them special and memorable. See below for some suggestions.

California

- **APRIL TO JUNE:** The best season to see coastal wildflowers.

- **JUNE TO SEPTEMBER:** The weather is warmest and sunniest. However, it's also peak travel season—prices for accommodations may be higher, the roads will be busier, and campsites will book up quickly.

- **NOVEMBER TO FEBRUARY:** A colder and slower season but the perfect time to spot migrating whales offshore and to see monarch butterflies, as the population size is at its height from the end of November through early December. Butterflies linger until the end of February.

Oregon

- **APRIL TO JUNE:** A great time to see blooming wildflowers, and it's a little quieter than peak season, but the weather can be finicky.

- **JULY TO AUGUST:** The summer weather is more predictable, but inland heat may cause coastal fog, which can limit your views of the ocean.

- **SEPTEMBER TO OCTOBER:** September typically has the best weather.

- **DECEMBER TO MARCH:** During the winter, many places in Oregon offer great chances to see migrating whales; peak times are mid-December through January and late March.

Washington

- **JULY TO SEPTEMBER:** These are the sunniest months to visit, although even at the height of summer, there can always be a little precipitation.

- **OCTOBER TO NOVEMBER:** Autumn, and even sometimes late autumn, can offer bits of beautiful sunny weather and vibrant fall colors. If you like hiking, it's a good time to enjoy Olympic National Park when it's a little quieter and before the snow comes.

CHAPTER 1

Southern California

Welcome to
SOUTHERN CALIFORNIA

Southern California is a wonderland of eternal summer. I have a deep love for this region, inspired by the countless waving palms, the pastel hues of sunsets, the ever-present mid-century design, the casual lifestyle that comes from a life lived in proximity to the waves.

As a kid who grew up in the 1990s, I saw California endlessly glorified in pop culture: *Beverly Hills, 90210*; *Saved by the Bell*; *Clueless*. It was a place I felt I knew, a place I wanted to be a part of. Many years later, I road-tripped across the country with a friend who was moving to Mammoth Lakes. As we rolled toward the Southern California coast, the sun was setting, the palm trees silhouetted against a purple sky. I remember us running to the freezing-cold water and dipping our toes in the Pacific Ocean for the first time. Those colors and emotions keep bringing me back.

I'm not the only one. For decades, this region has drawn artists, writers, musicians, and film directors from near and far, inspiring everything from the vivacious paintings of David Hockney to the poignant writings of Joan Didion. The sun-kissed views framed by a blue sky, warm air imbued with salt from the sea, fibrous palm tree trunks topped with dark green leaves; it all creates an intoxicating, irresistible blend.

The section of the Pacific coast that begins in San Diego and ends in San Luis Obispo takes you through legendary surf spots, beachside towns, historic landmarks, and even the urban metropolis of Los Angeles if you're craving a detour for a city adventure. You'll pass through towns like Del Mar, where succulents dot the side of the road. Beach bungalows in San Clemente are surrounded by cacti taller than their roofs. On the road, VW vans with surfboards on top dot the many pull-offs along the coastline. Boho-chic boutiques, cafés, and surf shacks line Highway 1 as you make your way up through Orange County and into the LA traffic grid.

California is home to more plant species than any other state, and the southern part of the coast is where you'll find native plants like California sagebrush, California morning glory, and chaparral yucca, all worth a stop for a photo or two. The flowers here are so vibrant that they seem to glow, and the air is filled with the scents of jasmine and eucalyptus.

The Pacific Coast Highway is lined with long stretches of sandy beaches—Huntington, Malibu, Salt Creek, Rincon—the waves attracting surfers from sunrise to sunset. While the outdoor pursuits of choice here revolve around the water, there is also ample opportunity for hiking and nature walks.

Besides the scenery, there's plenty to get you to pull the car over and make an impromptu stop. As you weave your way in and out of coastal towns, fresh food tempts from one of the many fruit stands or Mexican joints. For distinct souvenirs, there are vintage shops selling an array of funky mid-century homewares, clothing and eclectic jewelry, handmade ceramics, and Asian antiques.

Warm, sunny mornings spent overlooking the ocean, iced coffee in hand, afternoon stops to stick your feet in the silky sand, evening meals of tacos and margaritas topped off with purple-pink sunsets—can it get any better?

CALIFORNIA DREAMING

SAN DIEGO → SAN LUIS OBISPO
341 miles
7 hours (without stops)
5-8 days

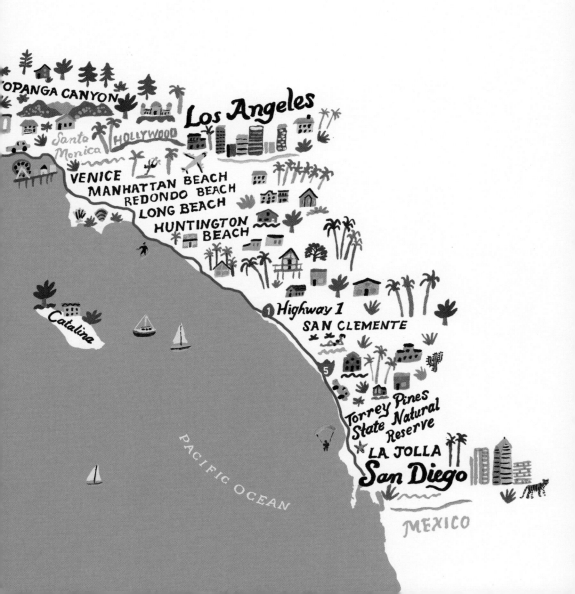

TOPANGA CANYON

Los Angeles

HOLLYWOOD

Santa Monica

VENICE

MANHATTAN BEACH

REDONDO BEACH

LONG BEACH

HUNTINGTON BEACH

Catalina

Highway 1

SAN CLEMENTE

Torrey Pines State Natural Reserve

LA JOLLA

San Diego

PACIFIC OCEAN

MEXICO

Destinations

SAN DIEGO ZOO

Every year, 3.2 million people from around the world flock here, making it the most popular zoo in America. The zoo is home to 3,500 animals, many of them rare and endangered. Peach flamingos greet you at the entrance, welcoming you to a world that's fun for adults and kids alike. Wander through the aviaries, walk the Monkey Trail, wave to the marsupials of the Outback, and discover the more than 700,000 exotic plants that grow throughout the zoo. Be prepared to do a lot of walking, and pack your lunch to avoid the overpriced food court.

LA JOLLA

From San Diego, take I-5 north for 16 miles to La Jolla. In 1894, a German woman named Anna Held established the Green Dragon Colony, welcoming artists, musicians, and writers from around the world. The colony and its cottages no longer exist, but La Jolla's arts scene holds strong with numerous galleries and festivals. Part of the city of San Diego, La Jolla sits right on the cliffs overlooking the Pacific Ocean. The rocky shores at the **La Jolla Tide Pools** are your first chance to find coastal marine life, like sea anemones, sculpins, and sinewy seaweed. Be sure to stroll along the bluffs on the **La Jolla Coast Walk Trail**. About a mile round-trip, this is said to have been a Native American hunting trail. Today the trail takes you past a string of beaches, with plenty of opportunities to spot sea lions bathing in the sun, kayakers off the shores, and upscale mid-century houses overlooking the ocean. **La Jolla Cove** is a nice spot for swimming and snorkeling. From here, it's a short walk to La Jolla's downtown area, full of restaurants, shops, and galleries.

Driving along the coastal highway

TORREY PINES STATE NATURAL RESERVE

About a fifteen-minute drive north of La Jolla, Torrey Pines State Natural Reserve is one of the wildest stretches of land on the Southern California coast. The protected 1,500 acres that make up the reserve offer a sense of what the landscape looked like before it was developed. Watch the hang gliders launch from the Gliderport lookout (or try hang gliding yourself). Hike the **Torrey Pines Beach Trail Loop** for canyon views and a walk along the shore. Remember your hat and sunscreen, as trails here are fully exposed to the sun.

From Torrey Pines, continue north on the coastal road, Camino Del Mar, for a slow-paced scenic detour, or hop onto I-5 if you're pressed for time.

TIDE POOL ETIQUETTE

Tide pools are pockets of water that remain in the craggy rocks after the tide pulls out. This is a precious area where plants and marine life thrive. It's a wondrous world that you can spend hours exploring, but enjoy it with care—here are some guidelines.

- **LOOK UP THE TIDE TABLE ONLINE BEFORE LEAVING.** You'll be able to find tide pools only at low tide, when the water recedes.

- **WEAR PROPER FOOTWEAR.** No flats or heels. I usually wear good-grip hiking sneakers. You can also wear rugged sandals.

- **WALK ONLY ON BARE ROCKS AND SAND.** Don't step on seaweed, mussels, or barnacles. Tiny sea creatures make their homes here, and you could squish them. And seaweed is extremely slippery.

- **DON'T DISTURB THE CREATURES.** Stand still next to the tide pool for a little while to see if there are any critters in it. Your presence can make them hide, but if you watch patiently, they will emerge and continue about their merry way.

- **BE PATIENT.** Don't expect to find everything you seek in one tide pool or even at one beach. Hop around and check out as many tide pools as are safe to access. You'll find that each one is unique.

- **PAY ATTENTION.** Don't turn your back on the ocean. Particularly in the Pacific Northwest, watch out for "sneaker waves," giant, sudden waves that unexpectedly consume areas that were totally dry moments before. Always be aware of your surroundings.

- **RESPECT THE WILDLIFE.** Don't touch anything in the tide pools or remove anything from them. If you really want to know what it's like to touch an anemone, there are aquariums and marine centers on the coast with touch tanks.

THINGS TO LOOK FOR IN A TIDE POOL

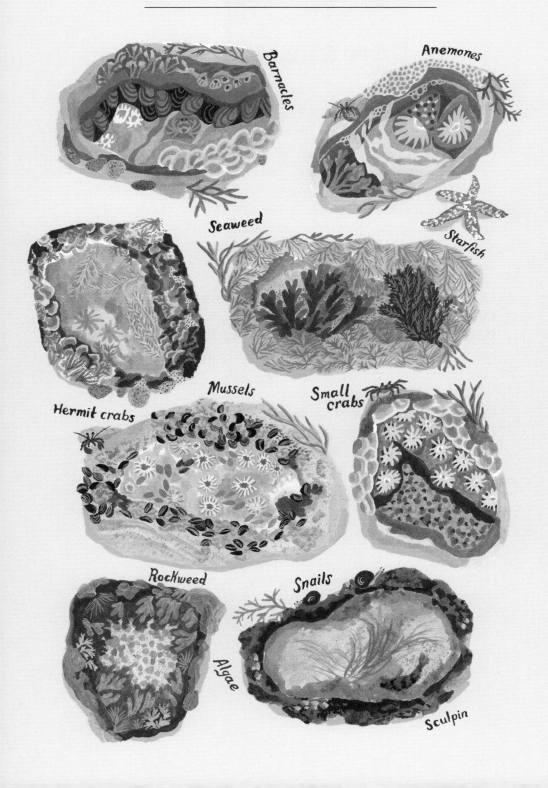

Barnacles

Anemones

Starfish

Seaweed

Hermit crabs

Mussels

Small crabs

Rockweed

Snails

Algae

Sculpin

SAN CLEMENTE

It's a 43-mile drive from Torrey Pines to San Clemente. In the 1920s, Ole Hanson, the founder of the city of San Clemente, and previously the mayor of Seattle, began working on the development of a "Spanish village by the sea" that would attract people looking to escape Los Angeles. San Clemente is renowned for its perpetual sunny weather (about 300 days a year) and local surf scene. Walk down Avenida del Mar and El Camino Real for boutiques, antiques shops, cafés, and restaurants. Just outside town, the **Surfing Heritage and Culture Center** is a great place to learn about surf history and see a vast collection of surfboards.

From here, drive back to the coastline and park at **Calafia Beach**, **San Clemente Pier Beach**, or **North Beach** to walk along the **San Clemente Beach Trail**, a 2-mile trail that strings all the local beaches together. Bring a blanket and watch the sunset as the locals light bonfires and play one last game of volleyball.

Casa Romantica Cultural Center and Gardens
Historic cultural center Casa Romantica is housed in Ole Hanson's original Spanish Colonial home. The building was used as inspiration for the rest of the San Clemente development, and for a small entrance fee, you can walk around terraced gardens and explore the grandiose home overlooking the ocean. Find a bench on the open terrace and listen to the waves below.

About 7 miles north of San Clemente is Dana Point, the start of Highway 1—commonly referred to as the Pacific Coast Highway, and also called Cabrillo Highway, Shoreline Highway, or Coast Highway on street signs—which runs almost 660 miles along the coast before ending in Leggett, California.

Casa Romantica →

OUTSKIRTS OF LOS ANGELES

Los Angeles can feel like one big continuous sprawl. Whether you're bypassing Los Angeles entirely or just taking a break before heading into the city, as Highway 1 sneaks along the coast from Orange County into Los Angeles County, stop at one of these beaches.

Huntington Beach

Nicknamed Surf City, USA, Huntington Beach is a world-class surf destination and boasts 10 miles of uninterrupted coastline.

Long Beach

About 25 miles south of Los Angeles, Long Beach is one of the world's busiest seaports. You'll find the **Aquarium of the Pacific**, Southern California's largest aquarium, and plenty of beach access.

Redondo Beach

Walk the **Redondo Pier**, where you'll find a string of seafood restaurants and a statue of George Freeth, the father of modern surfing. The soft sand here is perfect for a nap.

Manhattan Beach

Manhattan Beach is a laid-back beach community with a small downtown. **The Marvin Braude Bike Trail**, also known as the Strand, runs along the shore here, passing by mid-century beachfront houses and countless beachgoers. The waves are teeming with surfers, and the sand is sprinkled with tiny shells. Street parking is hard to come by, so head straight to a parking lot and avoid the competitive hunt for a spot.

VENICE

Venice is a short drive from Manhattan Beach. Initially founded as a beachside resort town, today Venice is eclectic and vibrant with a legendary boardwalk, a renowned skate park, and distinct local charm. Walk down the **Venice Beach Boardwalk** to enter a whirlwind of weird. Stretching for about a mile and a half along the coast, the boardwalk is Venice's central element, and a top tourist destination. At the shops along the boardwalk, you will find everything from bedazzled booty shorts and henna tattoos to knockoff shades and CBD gummies. Grab a snack from one of the vendors, and hang around to watch a few street performances. At the north end, find your way to the skate park on the beach, where you'll see local skaters zooming around the bowls. The graffiti and bohemian boardwalk culture are contrasted by the curated high-priced clothing and lifestyle boutiques on Abbot Kinney Boulevard, which runs diagonally inland. From here, it's about a fifteen-minute stroll over to the **Venice Canals**, where you can walk through the few remaining canals, originally constructed in an attempt to make the area the "Venice of America." Parking in Venice is limited, so either pay for parking by the beach or find a spot removed from the action and walk into town.

MUSCLE BEACH

Finds at the Rose Bowl Flea Market

LOS ANGELES

The Hollywood Sign, **Rodeo Drive**, **Grauman's Chinese Theatre**, the **Capitol Records Building**: Los Angeles is a piece of Americana, a city known for its movie culture, diversity, and persistently sunny weather. While the city isn't directly on the coast, if you have never been, it's worth pulling yourself away from the ocean and heading inland. Way before the rise of Hollywood in the early 1900s, the area was inhabited by the Chumash people, who settled in the Los Angeles basin as far back as 8000 BCE. They were later displaced by the Tongva, and in 1781, Spanish governor Felipe de Neve officially founded the city, home to more than 4 million people today. That makes for a lot of traffic, which can be overwhelming. I suggest ditching the car and wandering through one of the city's 105 museums, like **LACMA** (Los Angeles County Museum of Art) in the Mid-Wilshire district, with works spanning 6,000 years. If you're looking for something more out of the ordinary, try the **Museum of Jurassic Technology**. If you happen to be in the area on the second Sunday of the month, take a drive slightly farther inland to Pasadena to peruse the rows and rows of antiques and used goods at the world-famous **Rose Bowl Flea Market**. When you've worked up an appetite, the city abounds with culinary options like tacos at **Guisados**. End your night with a cocktail and live music at the **Dresden**.

Matisse at the LACMA

MORE TO SEE IN L.A.

The Broad · the Griffith Observatory · the Hollywood Bowl ·
Huntington Gardens · the Los Angeles Conservancy ·
the Los Angeles Theatre · Rodeo Drive · the Watts Towers

*Hike up to the Griffith Observatory for a view of the city
and to see the Hollywood Sign in the distance.*

THE GETTY VILLA

From downtown LA, take I-10 west, past Santa Monica and its iconic pier, back to Highway 1, and continue north to the Getty Villa, a 20-mile drive. Perched on an oceanfront cliff nestled into the Santa Monica Mountain foothills, this former estate of oil tycoon J. Paul Getty is an homage to the world of antiquities. Having purchased his first work of art—a small terra-cotta sculpture—in 1939, Getty went on to become an avid art collector, eventually building the villa as a museum to showcase his treasures. The breathtaking gardens and grounds are modeled after Villa dei Papiri, an ancient Roman villa that was destroyed by the eruption of Vesuvius and rediscovered in the mid-1700s. The estate has several interior galleries filled with Greek, Roman, and Etruscan antiquities, covering 7,000 years of art. It's a good place for a photo shoot; you'll undoubtedly see some selfie sticks and visitors posing elegantly on the side of the elongated pool or next to a Grecian statue. Don't miss the video when you first walk in to get a brief history about the estate and Getty's passion for art collecting. Admission is free, but you have to pay for parking.

Trompe l'oeil murals, Italian marble, and sculptures line the path from the galleries into the Roman-style gardens.

TOPANGA CANYON

Take a scenic 5-mile drive along Topanga Canyon Boulevard away from the coast, through the oak trees, and into this small bohemian community. A stone's throw from Los Angeles, it became a popular place for artists to settle in the 1960s, and the area is surrounded by **Topanga State Park**, the world's largest wildland within the boundaries of a major urban city. In the heart of the chaparral-lined canyon, the eclectic town center of Topanga hosts small businesses like **Hidden Treasures**, a vintage clothing shop; an inn; a cozy café; and a general store. With its relaxed sense of creativity, untamed nature, and sage-infused mountain air, this is the perfect spot to find a rental home and spend the night. Bring groceries, cook a simple meal, and sit outside among the stars and good vibes. Wake up early and start the day with a hike in **Tuna Canyon Park** or Topanga State Park before heading back out on the road. Pack water and a brimmed hat for the mostly exposed trails. From here, the drive to Malibu is about twenty minutes along the coast.

The patio at Hidden Treasures

NATURAL DISASTERS

The stunning, often rugged Pacific coast is a constantly evolving landscape shaped by nature and her elements. The Pacific coastline has dealt with everything from mudslides to floods to wildfires, which in recent years have been exacerbated by climate change. The impact of these natural disasters can be tremendous. At the end of 2018, California experienced its deadliest and most destructive fire on record, the Camp Fire in Butte County. In all seasons, check local conditions and road reports to know which areas are safe to drive in and visit. As communities rebuild, be sensitive to their needs, and travel respectfully, remembering that you too have an impact on the places that residents call home.

MALIBU

Once defined by a more relaxed surf culture, today Malibu is known for the grandiose estates of billionaires and celebrities. But the area—called "the 'Bu" by locals—still retains some of that original beach-town charm. Stop to enjoy at least one (or two) of the beautiful beaches on your way through. Start a little south of the center of Malibu at **Carbon Beach** to gape at the most expensive homes in town. For activities off the sand, **Malibu Country Mart** offers tasty meal options and curated shopping experiences. After eating, visit the nearby **Malibu Pier** and **Malibu Lagoon**, and stop at the **Adamson House**, a historic villa right on the water, which offers a look into Malibu's history for a small fee. The house was built in 1929, and its craftsmanship, decorative tile, stained glass, and frescoes are just a few features that will transport you back in time.

MALIBU BEACHES

Enjoy Malibu's 21-mile stretch of sandy beaches and their attractions. Signs for "private property" abound, but the wet sand is always public property. Here are a few beaches worth checking out.

El Matador State Beach · Point Dume State Beach · Surfrider Beach · Zuma Beach

VENTURA

From Zuma Beach, drive north for about forty minutes on Highway 1, which merges with Highway 101 right before Ventura. With a picturesque harbor, an old-fashioned Main Street, a wooden pier, and beaches with epic surf conditions, Ventura has a vintage feel. Stop and stretch your legs at **Surfers Point**, which has a paved beach pathway lined with clusters of slender palm trees. Ventura is also the gateway to the **Channel Islands National Park**. This secluded archipelago of islands is accessible by boat from Ventura Harbor and is the perfect location to experience untouched nature and rare wildlife. **Santa Cruz Island** is the easiest island to get to in the park and great for a day trip or a memorable night of camping among eucalyptus trees and curious foxes (they'll scavenge your food if you leave it out!). The ride to and from the island takes about an hour each way. If you're lucky, you might see dolphins swimming along or a whale breaching in the distance. Back on the road, it's 30 miles to Santa Barbara.

Ventura Harbor

PALM TREES

The *Washingtonia filifera* (California fan palm) is the only type of palm native to the state, growing in protected desert oases. All other palms—including the slender Mexican fan palms that line Los Angeles's boulevards and much of Southern California's coastal villages—are imports. The proliferation of palms came from the gardening and landscaping frenzy of the turn of the twentieth century, when palms were planted for ornamental purposes. In 1931 alone, the City of Los Angeles planted more than 25,000 palm trees that are today reaching the end of their natural life span. As they die off, they will be replaced with native trees adapted to more arid conditions and that provide shade, changing the iconic Southern Californian silhouette as we know it.

SANTA BARBARA

Often called the "American Riviera," Santa Barbara is an incredibly picturesque part of the Southern California coastline and a pleasant section to drive through. In 1786, the **Santa Barbara Mission** was founded by Franciscan missionary Fermín Lasuén, and the town's Spanish colonial roots are apparent in the Mediterranean-style white stucco buildings topped with red tiles and the flourishing gardens that are woven through the city. Learn about native plants at the **Santa Barbara Botanic Garden**, which offers picnic tables, scenic walking trails, and sweeping views of the Santa Ynez Mountains. For a more eclectic experience, visit **Ganna Walska Lotusland**, a 37-acre botanical nirvana featuring a stunning cactus garden. During the spring months, the hillsides of Santa Barbara are covered in blooming orange California poppies. (For an immersive view of the wildflowers, head about 50 miles north of town to **Figueroa Mountain**, where you can access hiking trails.) Back down by the water, the scenic and dog-friendly **Arroyo Burro Beach County Park** is a great place to take a break from the road and watch the local pups play in the waves. End your day with authentic Mexican food, a margarita, and a sunset at the beach.

Ganna Walska Lotusland

CALIFORNIA MISSIONS

As far south as San Diego and as far north as Sonoma, there are twenty-one historic missions in California, all along El Camino Real, a portion of Highway 1. Starting in 1769, Spain established missions to claim land and spread Catholicism, often by violence and manipulation, to the Indigenous population. The structures represent some of the oldest and most beautiful architecture in California yet were sites of great oppression. **La Purísima Concepción**, in Lompoc, is a memorable mission to visit with frequent educational events. The preserved structures include the ornately painted chapel, and rustic rooms like a woodshop, ceramics studio, and weaving room, as well as the soldiers' barracks and priests' chambers. Other notable missions in Southern California include **Old Mission Santa Bárbara** and **Mission San Luis Obispo de Tolosa**. To learn more about the history surrounding the California missions, visit the California Missions Foundation (californiamissionsfoundation .org) and the California Native American Heritage Commission (nahc.ca.gov).

The interior of La Purísima Concepción

Old Mission Santa Bárbara, founded in 1786

THE MISSIONS ON EL CAMINO REAL
(LISTED FROM SOUTH TO NORTH)

San Diego de Alcalá

San Luis Rey de Francía

San Juan Capistrano

San Gabriel Arcángel

San Fernando Rey de España

San Buenaventura

Santa Bárbara

Santa Inés

La Purísima Concepcíon

San Luis Obispo de Tolosa

San Miguel Arcángel

San Antonio de Padua

Nuestra Señora de la Soledad

San Carlos Borroméo
de Carmelo

San Juan Bautista

Santa Cruz

Santa Clara de Asís

San José

San Francisco de Asís

San Rafael Arcángel

San Francisco Solano

LOMPOC FLOWER FIELDS

About 30 miles north of Santa Barbara, Highway 1 cuts inland at Gaviota and takes you toward the small town of Lompoc, known for its flower fields. The abundant flowers, like larkspur and stock, are commercially planted and generally bloom from April to September, but the best time to see them is May and June. Head out of town on Ocean Avenue to start your hunt for flowers. You can find the fields on the rugged roads between Central and Ocean Avenues. I found a gorgeous—and fragrant—field of sweet peas on Floradale Avenue. Union Sugar Avenue is the last road through the fields. The flower fields are privately owned, but you can photograph them from the side of the road. Continue north about an hour to San Luis Obispo. On the way, stop at some of the fantastic fruit and vegetable stands, like **Okui Strawberry and Fruit Stand** and **Rutiz Family Farms**. As you drive, you'll notice the landscape changing. Golden rolling hills with roaming cattle, orange groves, and patches of vineyards fill this section of the central California coast.

SEASONAL CALIFORNIA FRUITS

In a region that's known for sunshine, there's always fresh fruit available. Here are some common ones you will spot and when to enjoy them at their best.

APRICOTS
May through July

TOMATOES
July through September

GRAPEFRUIT
January through September

LEMONS
Year-round

PLUMS
May through September

HASS AVOCADOS
February through July

NAVEL ORANGES
January through April

PEACHES
May through September

STRAWBERRIES
April through October

CANTALOUPE
May through November

VALENCIA ORANGES
May through October

POMEGRANATES
September through November

SAN LUIS OBISPO

San Luis Obispo—locals call it San Luis—is a laid-back town roughly midway between Los Angeles and San Francisco. Pay a visit to the sixty-year-old **Madonna Inn**, a pink-chintz dreamland on the outskirts of town where cherubs hang from the ceiling amid ornate woodwork and masses of faux flowers. It's a fun place to have a meal or a drink, or to spend the night in one of the wonderfully kitschy themed rooms. Head west on Los Osos Valley Road and drive through the eucalyptus grove at **Montaña de Oro State Park** to get to **Spooners Cove**. Park at the top of the cove for access to the **Bluff Trail**. This easy and sunny hike offers wonderful views of the coast.

If your trip ends here, there is a regional airport in San Luis Obispo or, for more options, backtrack to Santa Barbara's airport.

The pool at the Madonna Inn

The LOVE NEST

The ROSE ROOM

The LUCKY ROCK ROOM

CHAPTER 2

Northern California

Welcome to
NORTHERN CALIFORNIA

As you make your way north to the Central and Northern coast, the buzz of Southern California starts to fade: The towns up here are less populated, houses tucked away in dark-green hillsides that plunge into the sea. Surfers are encased in heavy wet suits to tackle the coast's famous breaks. The air is saltier, cooler, fresher. Busy beaches give way to secluded coves hidden between cliffs. Coastal fog seeps in between the redwoods, diffused rays of sunlight highlighting the blankets of prehistoric ferns and moss on the forest floor.

Like many, I was drawn to this region by the legend of Big Sur. The first time I drove through, my friend and I spent just one day here, but what a day it was. Warning: You may have trouble keeping your eyes on the road. We were so enthralled by the view that we nearly drove our car into a cliffside. The drive to Big Sur is an integral part of the experience of seeing it. Because of coastal road closures, Big Sur can be difficult to reach, and cell service is hit-or-miss; sometimes your only connection to those at home is through a pay phone. At times the landscape might even feel prehistoric, with its sea stacks and cliffs created by waves that have crashed for millennia and redwood trees standing tall for hundreds, even thousands, of years. To walk these woods and these shores is to be reminded of the slow evolution of the natural world around you.

While the Northern California coast has a sense of quiet and solitude, the San Francisco Bay Area is a bustling metropolis with a population of 7 million. Residents often explore the coast and forests to the north and south, and there is an entire industry of small towns that thrive off these weekend visitors. In art-filled towns like Carmel and Mendocino, it's easy to see how local artists take inspiration from the sea and forests that define this landscape, and throughout some of the small towns that line the coast, you still get a sense of the bohemian spirit that defined San Francisco and its surrounding areas in the 1960s and '70s.

San Francisco is generally much cooler and grayer than Southern California; the area's warmest weather comes during autumn. I've found that it's helpful to stash a couple of extra layers of clothing in your car and take them with you on a hike, even if you start out in glorious sunshine.

Fog and hills make for a lush landscape, and Northern California is a rich agricultural region. Napa, Sonoma, and Mendocino are known for their sprawling vineyards; fresh oysters are pulled from Tomales Bay near Point Reyes National Seashore; and up and down the coast, farms of all kinds ensure a food culture rooted in local cuisine. It's no surprise that the farm-to-table movement was born here, spurred by the work of Alice Waters at Berkeley's Chez Panisse. There's an abundance of fresh, local food at San Francisco's Ferry Plaza Farmers Market, as well as at farmers' markets and stands in many of the small towns in the region.

As you inch your way closer to the Oregon border, the enormous coastal redwoods, *Sequoia sempervirens*, are nothing less than enchanting. Though they once covered millions of acres of land, logging has reduced the old-growth forests to a minuscule percentage of what they were. But these trees are resilient, and preservation efforts are in place so that generations to come will walk through these forests.

If you're ready to rise to the dewy morning smell of earth and fall asleep to the sound of hooting owls, feel the spray of salty air as it hits the headlands, and crane your neck to look up into the canopy of ancient forests, grab a layer and let's get going.

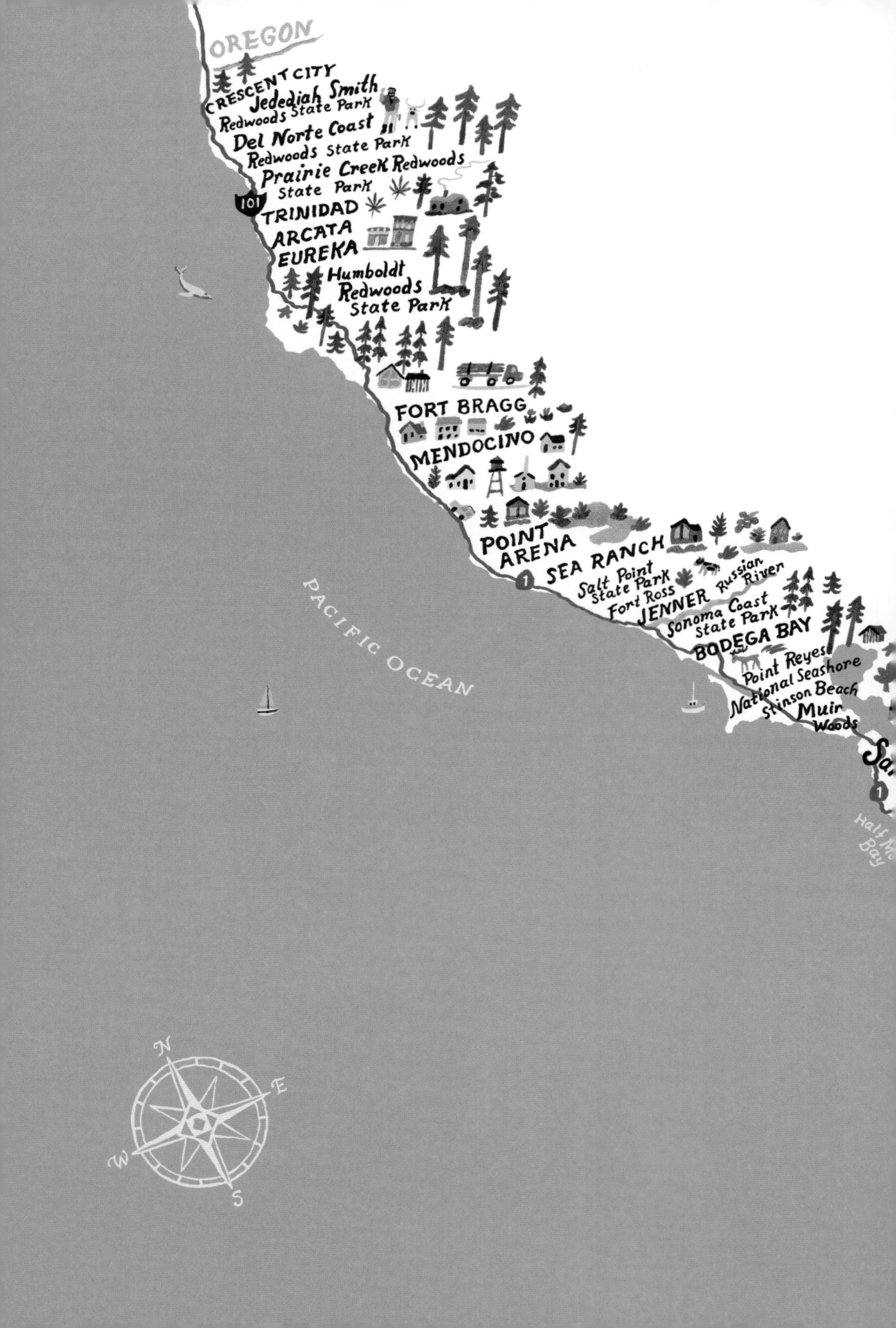

OREGON

CRESCENT CITY
Jedediah Smith
Redwoods State Park
Del Norte Coast
Redwoods State Park
Prairie Creek Redwoods
State Park
101 TRINIDAD
ARCATA
EUREKA
Humboldt
Redwoods
State Park

FORT BRAGG
MENDOCINO

POINT
ARENA
SEA RANCH
Salt Point
State Park
Fort Ross
JENNER Russian River
Sonoma Coast
State Park
BODEGA BAY
Point Reyes
National Seashore
Stinson Beach
Muir
Woods
Sa

PACIFIC OCEAN

1

Half Mo
Bay

N
E
W
S

SAN SIMEON → CRESCENT CITY
613 miles
14 hours (without stops)
8-10 days

Destinations

SAN SIMEON

About fifty minutes north of San Luis Obispo in San Simeon is **Hearst Castle**. The National Historic Landmark, originally constructed by William Randolph Hearst in the early twentieth century, is definitely worth a few hours of your time. The castle sits on 127 acres, and its 165 rooms are opulent and breathtaking. Book a $25 guided tour. The Grand Rooms tour is the most recommended by staff and takes around an hour. After the tour, roam the gardens on your own. Hearst also had the world's largest private zoo, which is no longer in operation, but if you see a few zebras grazing in the grass, you'll know why.

The Neptune Pool at Hearst Castle

Elephant Seal Vista Point

About 5 miles from Hearst Castle, stroll down the long coastal walkway to see elephant seals in their natural habitat. These entertaining creatures gather here to birth, and males compete with one another to impress the females. Between January and February, there are adorable newborn pups to spot; year-round, friendly volunteer guides walk around, answering questions and sharing stories of the elephant seals. There is ample parking, but it can get crowded. Stop at the **Friends of the Elephant Seal gift shop** south of the viewing point in San Simeon; all proceeds go to maintaining this special location.

BIG SUR

A magical intersection of waterfalls, cozy cottages, flower fields, redwoods, palm trees, sandy beaches, and rocky shores, the 90-mile stretch of coastline between Hearst Castle and Carmel-by-the-Sea known as Big Sur has attracted tourists since the 1950s. Here, nature appears unspoiled: fog blankets bluffs that extend into the water, redwood trees shoot up into the starry skies, and the Santa Lucia Mountains rise abruptly from the Pacific Ocean. The original inhabitants—the Esselen, Ohlone, and Salinan peoples—led a nomadic existence on the coast during warmer months and moved inland as it got colder. When Spanish explorers arrived in the sixteenth and seventeenth centuries, they named the area El País Grande del Sur, or the Big Country of the South. It remained hard to get to and mostly cut off from the rest of the region until the 1930s, when Highway 1 was built, with thirty-nine bridges traversing coastal canyons and cliffs, including the famous Bixby Bridge, an engineering marvel. Big Sur soon became a haven for artists, musicians, and bohemians seeking an escape and the inspiration that comes from a place of such natural beauty and solitude, leading to the opening of retreats like the **Esalen Institute**, where the hot springs have been used in rituals and healing for more than 6,000 years. Mostly reserved for visitors studying massage or meditation in one of the institute workshops, the hot springs are open for public bathing between 1 a.m. and 3 a.m., by online reservation only. There are plenty of campgrounds in the area, but be sure to book in advance. For indoor lodging, try **Glen Oaks Big Sur**, and enjoy cabins with gas fireplaces and outdoor firepits. At the historic **Deetjen's Big Sur Inn**, where there is no need for TV or Wi-Fi, you'll find a restaurant and comfortable, rustic rooms on the edge of the redwood forest.

Henry Miller Memorial Library

A nonprofit arts center, bookstore, and performance venue, the library in Big Sur champions the late writer and resident Henry Miller, as well as other local artists and writers. Check its events calendar to see if there is something happening while you're visiting. Otherwise, just stop in to browse the bookstore, play a game of Ping-Pong, and sip a coffee.

Nepenthe

Situated 808 feet above sea level, overlooking the ocean, on land originally purchased from Hollywood legends Orson Welles and Rita Hayworth, this restaurant in Big Sur was constructed with local materials like adobe and redwood to blend in with its surroundings. Stop in for a peek, or stay for a drink or a meal. If you're dining here, try to sit along the perimeter for the most unobstructed and breathtaking view. Don't miss the gift shop, which is packed with a selection of nature books and items made by local crafts-people. The parking lot is crowded, but be patient, as people are always flowing in and out.

BIG SUR CAMPGROUNDS

Big Sur is an ideal place to book a campsite. With the exception of Ponderosa and Nacimiento Campgrounds, which run on a first-come-first-serve basis, others reserve sites as far out as six months in advance, so keep that in mind if you're traveling during peak season. Here are some recommendations, listed from south to north.

Plaskett Creek Campground · Kirk Creek Campground · Ponderosa Campground · Nacimiento Campground · Limekiln State Park · Ventana Campground · Pfeiffer Big Sur Campground · Big Sur Campground & Cabins

BIG SUR HIKES

You could spend days, even weeks, hiking around Big Sur. Here are some of my favorite places to explore the trails.

- **SALMON CREEK FALLS.** A fairly easy fifteen-minute hike takes you to this cascading waterfall, where you can go for a dip in the chilly waters.

- **LIMEKILN STATE PARK.** For $10, you can explore plenty of short, beautiful hikes in this smaller park. The shaded Limekiln Creek Falls Trail takes you through redwoods, across streams, and to a waterfall. You can also visit the four limekilns it's named for.

- **PARTINGTON COVE.** You can get directly to this secluded cove by hiking down a steep hill, over a bridge, and through a 60-foot wooden tunnel. Wander down the offshoots to the left and right for a waterfall and a rocky beach.

- **JULIA PFEIFFER BURNS STATE PARK.** Some areas of this park, named after one of Big Sur's pioneers, are currently closed due to recent storm damage. However, McWay Falls, a breathtaking waterfall that trickles into the ocean, is still viewable off the road.

Limekiln State Park →

BIG SUR BEACHES

The beaches of Big Sur are hugged by the bluffs and cliffs that make for many panoramic vistas. Because of the steep cliffs, as well as private properties, much of the coastline is inaccessible to the public, but the beaches that you can get to are worth the effort. Here are some that I love.

- **JADE COVE.** You have to hike down a treacherous cliff, and while it's not guaranteed that you'll spot any jade, the cove is gorgeous and a gem in and of itself.

- **SAND DOLLAR BEACH.** A steep climb down takes you to this secluded little beach right off Highway 1. Rocks jut out on the shores, and kelp sways in the water. If you can't snag a spot on the street to park, there is $10 parking (cash only).

- **PFEIFFER BEACH.** A short walk takes you to maybe the most easily accessible beach in Big Sur, a peaceful alcove with a lagoon and a natural rock archway. Bring your lunch and stay awhile, or come to catch the sunset. It costs $10 (cash) to park.

- **ANDREW MOLERA STATE PARK.** A pleasant 1.5-mile hike leads you to this windswept beach with several driftwood shelters. It's a nice spot to cozy up and watch the waves roll in. Bring an extra layer, as the beach gets chilly. It costs $10 (cash) to park.

Sticky monkey flower

Forget-me-not

Calla lily

Osteospermum

Redwood sorrel

Wild poppy

Morning glory

Blue witch

WILDFLOWERS

May is wildflower month in California, and Big Sur explodes with flowers that bloom until early summer. Monterey County has more than 2,300 different species of wildflowers, in more than 140 families.

RESPECTING MOTHER NATURE

It's a privilege to be able to experience natural areas like the Pacific coast that are wild, untouched, and well preserved. No matter where you are—whether it's a crowded beach in Southern California or a quiet forest in Oregon—follow these guidelines.

- **ALWAYS PACK OUT YOUR TRASH.** To go a step further, pick up litter even if it doesn't belong to you and discard it properly.

- **DO NOT GRAFFITI ON ROCKS OR CARVE INTO TREES.** Even just one stab into the side of a tree will make it more vulnerable to disease and may ultimately cause the tree to die.

- **FORAGE ONLY WHAT YOU KNOW.** Berries and mushrooms thrive along this coastline, but don't pick and eat them unless you're 100 percent confident of the identification. Also, refer to local park and property rules on foraging.

- **DON'T GET TOO CLOSE TO THE EDGE OF A CLIFF.** Respect fences and guardrails—the geography of the coast is always changing, and these areas can be dangerous.

- **STAY ON THE TRAIL.** Not only does trampling off route negatively impact the local flora and fauna, but also poison oak grows abundantly in the wilderness, and you don't want to be bushwhacking through it.

- **NEVER FEED WILD ANIMALS.** If we continue to give wild animals food, they'll acclimate and rely on our handouts, hurting their chances for survival in their natural habitat. Additionally, they'll become more confident about approaching humans, which may lead to attacks.

- **USE A MAP.** At the trailhead, look for a trail map to take with you, or snap a picture of it. This will also give you a time-stamped reference for when you started the hike.

- **CHECK YOURSELF FOR TICKS.** After you have spent time in any woody, grassy, or brushy areas, give yourself a good once-over.

THE CALIFORNIA POPPY

Designated the state flower in 1903, the bright orange California poppy (*Eschscholzia californica*) actually grows from southern Washington all the way down to Mexico's Baja California. During the spring and summer, when the poppies bloom, coastal hillsides light up with the intense color. It's no wonder that early Spanish settlers called this poppy *copa de oro* (cup of gold). Historically, natives used the California poppy to ease aches and pains. It's still used medicinally, in tincture form, as a pain reliever and gentle sedative. Unlike the opium poppy, the California poppy is not addictive.

COMMON NORTHERN CALIFORNIA PLANTS

Sagebrush

California sagebrush is considered one of the most medicinally useful plants, long employed by Native Americans to combat a range of ailments, most notably as a natural remedy for colds. The antimicrobial nature of its leaves lends itself well to keeping foods fresh and uncontaminated. It is also very aromatic.

Poison Oak

Flourishing in late spring and early summer, particularly after heavy storms, poison oak can grow as a creeper, a climber, or an ordinary shrub. All parts of the plant secrete an oily resin, which will cause an extremely itchy rash. Remember the old Girl Scouts mnemonic "Leaves of three, let it be."

Yarrow

Native Americans used yarrow to relieve pain and reduce fever (it contains salicylic acid, the active ingredient in aspirin), to treat cuts and colds, and as a sleep aid.

California Wild Rose

This beautiful and resilient native rose species grows along the coast and foothills of California, and in the mountains up to elevations of 6,000 feet.

Ice Plant

A coastal succulent also known as a sea fig, this nonnative invasive plant carpets the coastal walkway of Pacific Grove in bright magenta hues in April and May.

Eucalyptus Tree

Native to southeastern Australia, eucalyptus trees came to California in the 1850s during the Gold Rush. Their fragrant oils make them highly vulnerable to fire, and they are considered invasive because they compete with native plants. In some places, monarch butterflies love to congregate on the trees in huge numbers during their winter migrations.

Monterey Cypress

Native to the Monterey peninsula, some of these trees have survived centuries of hot weather, nurtured by coastal fog and whipped by the ocean wind into tortured and sinewy shapes.

CARMEL-BY-THE-SEA

You'll know you're leaving Big Sur when you drive over the famous **Bixby Bridge**, built in 1932. Stop for a picture and a last wistful glance before rejoining the road, making your way through **Garrapata State Park** and into Carmel, about a twenty-minute drive. On the south end of the Monterey Peninsula, before the topography juts out into the Pacific Ocean, sits Carmel-by-the-Sea. The "sea" is of course so self-evident that locals just call the city Carmel. The **Carmel Mission**, which you can still visit today, was established in 1771, but it wasn't until the early 1900s that modern-day Carmel took form. The town soon became a haven for artists, fueled by the early work of Jane Gallatin Powers and her husband, Frank Powers, who hosted salons at their home, attracting the creative class of San Francisco. In 1910, the *Los Angeles Times* deemed Carmel a "hotbed of soulful culture." Today it has become a wealthy enclave for those looking to escape the city, but its artistic roots still run deep—there are nearly a hundred art galleries within one square mile.

Point Lobos

Garrapata State Park

Colorful flowering succulents speckle the hillside in this park where the trails wind from the ocean into redwood groves. A short steep hike takes you down to the picturesque beach, persuading beachgoers to stay for a lazy afternoon.

Point Lobos State Natural Reserve

This park is considered the crown jewel of the California state park system. Watch whales in winter and sea lions all year round, hike the trails, go bird-watching, or even scuba dive. The park is also the home of the **Whaler's Cabin**. Built in 1851 by Chinese fishermen, it's a tiny bit of California history, having survived the many incarnations of the area, from a locus of the whaling industry to an abalone cannery to a coal mine operation to a gravel quarry. The cabin even served as the headquarters for the US Army Coastal Defense Squad just after Pearl Harbor. At the adjacent **Whaling Station Museum**, the only on-site whaling museum on the West Coast, you can dive a little deeper into the area's history, exploring the impressive array of artifacts and the whalebone graveyard outside.

*The whalebone graveyard
at the Whaling Station Museum*

Flying Waterbirds

PACIFIC GROVE

Fifteen minutes north of Carmel, visit the **Pacific Grove Museum of Natural History**, home to an eclectic collection of local taxidermy as well as fossil specimens and an assemblage of insects and butterflies—fascinating for adults and children alike. (Ask the staff about the scavenger hunt.) Don't miss the garden out back, which is full of native plants. Pacific Grove also happens to have the largest overwintering site of monarch butterflies in America; you can catch the winter migration at the **Monarch Sanctuary**, a short drive or a twenty-minute walk from the museum.

17-Mile Drive

Continuing north on Highway 1, pull off onto CA-68 to reach the 17-Mile Drive in Pacific Grove. A scenic detour off an already scenic highway, the views along this road, which meanders through **Pebble Beach**, are splendid no matter which stop you pull off at. At **Seal Rock** and **Bird Rock**, you can explore the tide pools. Access to the road and gated community costs $10. This area is also a popular golfing destination, so check the calendar to be sure there isn't a tournament going on if you want to avoid crowds.

Shepherd's Knoll

China Rock

Crocker Grove

Huckleberry Hill

Bird Rock

The Lone Cypress

The Inn and Links at Spanish Bay

Seal Rock

The Ghost Tree

Spanish Bay

The Restless Sea

Fanshell Overlook

The Lodge at Pebble Beach

Cypress Point Lookout

Stops along the 17-Mile Drive

MONTEREY

Located a stone's throw from Carmel, previously the center of the sardine-packing industry, Monterey bustles with gift shops, antiques stores, seafood restaurants, and bars in converted factories. The town center is found at Cannery Row, where turn-of-the-twentieth-century canneries sit overlooking the water. Originally called Ocean View Avenue, the street was officially renamed in honor of John Steinbeck's novel, which was set against the backdrop of this area. Today the historic charm of Monterey is intact, and it's a perfect place to stroll through and take in the sea air. It can easily get congested, so consider parking a little farther out, like at **Lovers Point** in Pacific Grove, a twenty-five-minute walk on the coastal pathway to Monterey. At **Lovers Point State Marine Reserve**, you might spot sea lions basking on the shore. Peruse the many treasures, including a vast collection of jewelry, nautical and Asian antiques, and collectible glass reminiscent of the jellyfish in the aquarium, at the **Cannery Row Antique Mall**, a two-floor mall in one of the old cannery buildings with more than a hundred vendors. Keep your eye out for miniature snuff bottles, brought over by Chinese émigrés in the nineteenth century.

Cannery Row Pier

Monterey Bay Aquarium

At this world-famous aquarium, there are more than 35,000 creatures in almost 200 exhibits, including a 28-foot-tall kelp forest. It's nearly impossible to see everything in one day, so choose which exhibits to prioritize. Ticket prices aren't cheap, but the cost is well worth it.

The jellies and anemones exhibits

WEST OF THE WEST

The Brave Wild Coast   JUDSON CREWS

BIG SUR AND THE ORANGES
OF HIERONYMOUS BOSCH   Henry Miller

JOAN DIDION Where I Was From

ARCHITECTURE OF THE SOUTHWEST

Monterey antiques store

CAPITOLA

About an hour from Monterey is Capitola, known as California's oldest
coastal resort town. Originally set up as a beachside tent camp in 1874, it
soon became known as a summer vacation destination for those wishing to
escape the scorching inland heat. The town has maintained its laid-back
resort vibe, but instead of tents, the shores of Capitola are now lined with
colorful homes, shops, and restaurants.

SANTA CRUZ

Santa Cruz, a short drive from Capitola, epitomizes the laid-back West Coast beach town vibe. Downtown is small and easy to explore on foot. The main attraction is the **Santa Cruz Beach Boardwalk**, with California's oldest amusement park (opened in 1907) still going strong today. Ride its famous wooden roller coaster and carousel, play games on the boardwalk, and enjoy carnival food, like deep-fried Twinkies. Be sure to take some keepsake photos in the arcade photo booths.

If a busy boardwalk isn't your scene, head to **Seabright State Beach** for a calmer experience. To get there, walk the rickety bridge across the San Lorenzo River or find a safer pathway at Riverside Avenue. Indulge in homemade ice cream at mom-and-pop shop **Marianne's Ice Cream**.

Santa Cruz is designated a World Surfing Reserve, and whether you get in the waves or not, you can learn about the history of surf culture at the **Santa Cruz Surfing Museum**. Covering a century of Santa Cruz surf culture, the museum is housed in a preserved lighthouse perched on a cliff. See if you can spot surfers braving the waves in the waters down below.

From downtown Santa Cruz, it's about ten minutes to the **Natural Bridges State Beach**. Try to time it so you're overlooking the natural arched rock formation by sunset. Nearby in **Wilder Ranch State Park**, hike the Old Cove Landing Trail to the Ohlone Bluff Trail for cliffside views. There's a free tour of the Victorian home and ranch on the site.

CALIFORNIA SURF HISTORY

While surf culture may seem synonymous with California, the sport has its roots in Polynesia and Hawaii. Surfing came to California in 1885, when three Hawaiian princes who were studying in California came to Santa Cruz and surfed on boards made from redwood that they had ordered from the local timber mill. In the early 1900s, George Freeth, credited with reviving the traditional Polynesian sport in Hawaii, came to California and earned the title of "Father of Modern Surfing." In 1926, lifeguard Tom Blake was the first to surf at Malibu, and he later developed the hollow surfboard. By 1950, surfboards had evolved from wood to fiberglass, and the California surf culture continued to grow. Jack O'Neill, who had opened the O'Neill Surf Shop in Santa Cruz in 1952, created the modern neoprene wet suit as a way to extend surfing seasons in the cooler Northern California waters. In the 1970s, a group of female surfers rode the waves at the Pro Tour and became known as the California Golden Girls. Today surfing is California's official state sport.

OUTSKIRTS OF SAN FRANCISCO

Take Highway 1 twenty minutes north of Santa Cruz and arrive at **Swanton Berry Farm**, the oldest organic strawberry farm in California. Then as Highway 1 approaches San Francisco, there is an abundance of places worth your time. Fill up the tank and pick up some tasty Mexican food at gas station/eatery **Mercado & Taqueria de Amigos**, and have a picnic at **Pescadero State Beach**. Look for sea anemones, crabs, hermit crabs, and guppies. **Half Moon Bay** offers a brewery, a distillery, and impressive tide pools at **Fitzgerald Marine Preserve**. Cut inland on CA-92 and stop at **Filoli**, a European-style garden with manicured shrubs, reflecting pools, and gorgeous mountain vistas. From here, San Francisco is about thirty minutes away.

Filoli Garden

Swanton Berry Farm truck

SAN FRANCISCO

A hilly city full of Victorian charm, history, and quirkiness, San Francisco today attracts free spirits and tech execs alike. Originally a Spanish mission, it was acquired by the United States in 1846. An invading army of prospectors moved in several years later, upon the discovery of gold in the region. The Gold Rush made San Francisco a cosmopolitan metropolis. This resilient city, which has survived several devastating earthquakes and fires, has maintained its reputation as a flourishing cultural bohemia through the decades. It drew in writers like Mark Twain and Jack London, and became a center for Beat poets in the 1950s. The Haight-Ashbury hippie movement peaked with the 1967 "Summer of Love," drawing in musicians like Jimi Hendrix, the Grateful Dead, and Janis Joplin. San Francisco was host to another subculture movement in the late 1970s and early 1980s: the rising punk scene, including local act Dead Kennedys. If you can, reserve a few days for this city because there is plenty to see. For those just passing through, Highway 1 runs directly past Golden Gate Park and the Presidio, both of which are great for getting a small dose of the city. San Francisco's hills make walking around a challenge; it's best to travel by car or one of the historic trolleys.

Golden Gate Park

Spanning fifty blocks, Golden Gate Park contains the **de Young art museum** and the **California Academy of Sciences**. Walk through the delightfully colorful and fragrant Rose Garden on your way to or from the museums (the garden is in bloom from May to September). For more botanicals, make your way to the **Conservatory of Flowers**, located in a Victorian greenhouse. The outdoor Dahlia Garden, an amazing display of San Francisco's official flower, starts blooming in June. Also in the park is the **Japanese Tea Garden**, with stepping-stone paths, koi ponds, pagodas, pruned trees, native Japanese plants, and a half-circle "moon bridge." Enjoy a cup of warm tea and a light meal at the traditional teahouse.

The iconic Victorian houses of San Francisco

The Presidio

For 218 years, the Presidio was an army post; it is now part of the National Park Service with 24 miles of trails, including the **Batteries to Bluffs Trail**, which guides you along the cliffs bordering the Pacific Ocean, past historic gun batteries and stunning vistas. Pull over at the **Golden Gate Overlook** for a glimpse of the **Golden Gate Bridge**, built in 1937 to connect San Francisco to Marin County. For expansive views from the bridge, head to the Golden Gate Bridge Welcome Center to start your windy walk en plein air. Visit the **Walt Disney Family Museum** for a dive back into your childhood. The museum houses a collection of memorabilia and original concept art from early Disney movies. Classic animations are screened daily in a small theater. On the eastern edge of the park, walk through the grounds at the **Palace of Fine Arts**. With its romantic atmosphere, reflecting pool, and grand Roman architecture, you'll feel as if you've stepped back into ancient Italy.

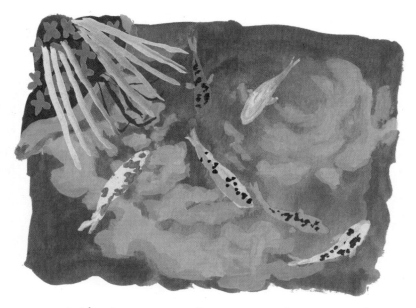

Koi at the Japanese Tea Garden in Golden Gate Park

East of the Presidio lies **Fisherman's Wharf**, originally where nineteenth-century Italian fishermen brought their daily catch to be sold and today a busy tourist destination. You can still enjoy fresh seafood, right out of the bay, at the many stands along the wharf, which serve clams, oysters, mussels, and chowder in a sourdough bread bowl. You can ride on an old-timey cable car at Taylor and Bay Streets, or just pose in front of one. Save your quarters for the **Musée Mécanique**, a quirky museum packed with working vintage arcade machines and photo booths. Explore the bay on one of the many boat tours before getting back on the road.

Golden Gate Bridge

MORE TO SEE IN SAN FRANCISCO

The Alamo Drafthouse Cinema · Chinatown · Coit Tower ·
Dolores Park · the Ferry Plaza Farmers Market · Haight-
Ashbury · the Legion of Honor museum · the Mission District ·
the San Francisco Museum of Modern Art · Twin Peaks

MUIR WOODS

From the Golden Gate Bridge, it takes about forty minutes to get to Muir Woods. During the Gold Rush, local forests were decimated to supply building materials for the burgeoning city of San Francisco. In an attempt to save at least a section of the redwoods, Marin County conservationist and congressman William Kent bought 611 acres along Redwood Canyon in 1905. However, two years later, a local water company sued Kent in an attempt to condemn the canyon and put in a reservoir, so Kent requested help from President Theodore Roosevelt. With Roosevelt's support, the forest was named a national monument in 1908. Kent chose to honor renowned conservationist John Muir with its name. Today Muir Woods is so popular, you need to reserve a time slot online prior to arriving to enter the park. Easy trails run along the canyon floor, offering a dramatic perspective of the ancient trees; for a more challenging hike, try the **Canopy View Trail**, which takes you as high as the redwoods. You may notice a lack of bugs buzzing around. The redwoods are high in tannin, which is a natural insect repellent.

Bohemian Grove Trail at Muir Woods

Chipmunks

Mycenas

Coral fungi

Gem-studded puffballs

Red hygrophorus mushrooms

Wild fennel

STINSON BEACH

From Muir Woods, it's a little more than twenty minutes to Stinson Beach, part of the Golden Gate National Recreation Area and a popular place for San Francisco locals to escape the city. Stop in town at **Stinson Beach Books**, or at the **Siren Canteen** for Mexican fare served beachside. If your feet are restless, walk left along the shore to find starfish, anemones, and mussels clinging to sea stacks.

POINT REYES NATIONAL SEASHORE

Continue thirty minutes north on Highway 1 to the town of Point Reyes Station. Fuel up here before driving into Point Reyes National Seashore, a national park with more than 1,500 species of plants and animals. Plan to spend two to four hours here, as the drive to the lighthouse is about 40 miles round-trip from Point Reyes Station, not including any side trips you might take. There are almost 150 miles of hiking trails to explore. Or take it easy and enjoy the landscape by car, making sure to pass through the **Cypress Tree Tunnel** that leads to an old radio receiving station. Look for elephant seals at the **Point Reyes Headlands**, and during migration season, gray whales cruising by. **Point Reyes Lighthouse** is located at the end of Sir Francis Drake Boulevard, 308 steps down. It's known to be the windiest part of the coast, so bundle up.

Cypress Tree Tunnel →

BODEGA BAY

Bodega Bay is fifty minutes north of Point Reyes Station. Highway 1 runs along Tomales Bay, which is known for its excellent seafood. Protected by an arm of land that sticks out into the Pacific and looks out to the Bodega Head State Marine Reserve, Bodega Bay is where Alfred Hitchcock's classic *The Birds* was filmed. Drive inland to Bodega for a little Hitchcock history. Featured in the film, the **Potter Schoolhouse** was lovingly restored by the family who currently lives there. You can snap a photo, but be respectful of their private property and don't trespass. Stock up on treats for the road at the **Bodega Country Store** and **Patrick's Salt Water Taffy**. **Bodega Head** is a popular spot for whale watching, and for camping, try **Bodega Dunes**, **Wright's Beach**, or **Willow Creek**. **Chanslor Ranch** is a little more pricey than the state-owned campgrounds, but the campsites are private and exquisitely perched on the mountainside, making it worth the splurge.

Horseback riding at Chanslor Ranch

The Potter Schoolhouse from "The Birds"

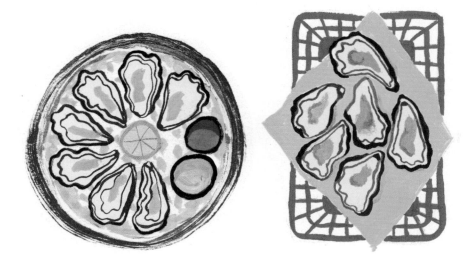

Legendary oysters from Tomales Bay restaurants

SONOMA COAST STATE PARK

Spanning 17 miles along the coast, from Bodega Bay to just north of Jenner, this is a great place for fishing, hiking, exploring, and relaxing. (Don't try to swim here, though—the water is rough and chilly.) Here are my top choices.

- **GLEASON BEACH.** A steep trail descends from the parking area to this narrow, rocky beach. It's best to visit at low tide when you can walk around the huge sea stacks.

- **SHELL BEACH.** As its name implies, this is a perfect place for beachcombing (see page 130). Accessible by a short hike down a steep path, it's also a great place to explore tide pools, but it can be slippery when wet, so wear sturdy shoes.

- **KORTUM TRAIL.** Starting at Shell Beach, this 4.5-mile (one way) bluff-top trail takes you through the coastal prairie, much of it along a double-plank wooden walkway that traverses the wetlands. You'll be rewarded with sweeping views of the ocean and the offshore sea stacks. At multiple points, you can veer off to one of the beaches, or up the trailside rock outcroppings. The trail ends at Goat Rock, or earlier if you're getting tired, then you'll walk back the way you came.

- **POMO CANYON TRAIL.** Also starting from Shell Beach, this trail runs 6.5 miles inland on a round-trip loop. As you walk, you'll see crashing waves, wildflowers, rolling hills, the redwoods, and a grand view of the Russian River. For both this hike and the Kortum Trail, come prepared with sunscreen, water, food, and a warm layer.

- **GOAT ROCK BEACH.** Turn down Goat Rock Road. When you get to the fork, turn right for the shores of the Russian River estuary; turn left for a rocky beach on the ocean.

RUSSIAN RIVER

Take a detour inland along the Russian River and experience Sonoma County firsthand. The river was originally known as Ashokawna, or "east water place," in the Southern Pomo indigenous language. Its current name comes from the Russian-American Company, with its settlement at Fort Ross (see page 104). Flowing a total of 110 miles, the river feeds into the Pacific Ocean at Jenner, where you can follow CA-116 inland to Healdsburg for about an hour, passing through several tiny towns and likely encountering misty, forested backdrops. Stop and stretch your legs at Guerneville. Don't miss the **Guerneville 5 & 10**, an eclectic shop where you'll find toys, incense, postcards, puzzles, kites, and water tubes, perfect for floating on the river in the warmer months.

One of the many vineyards along the Russian River

FORT ROSS

The drive from Jenner, at the mouth of the Russian River, to Fort Ross takes twenty-five minutes. In the early to mid-1800s, this was Russia's southernmost fur-trading outpost in North America. The isolated park, propped on a cliff overlooking the ocean, features original fortress walls and structures. The park hosts cultural festivals celebrating Russian heritage several times a year; check its calendar of events for details. Even if nothing special is going on, this is a beautiful place to linger.

SALT POINT
STATE PARK

In an area that once boasted several active sawmills, today Salt Point State Park, located fifteen minutes north of Fort Ross, offers breathtaking bluff trail hikes. The hikes are mostly flat and lead you to one beautiful cove after another. Sandstone from Salt Point helped to build the streets of San Francisco. Look for the "tafoni," the park's distinct honeycomb-textured rocks. Though there are theories that this unique rock art was formed by salt weathering and burrowing mollusks, its real origins remain a mystery.

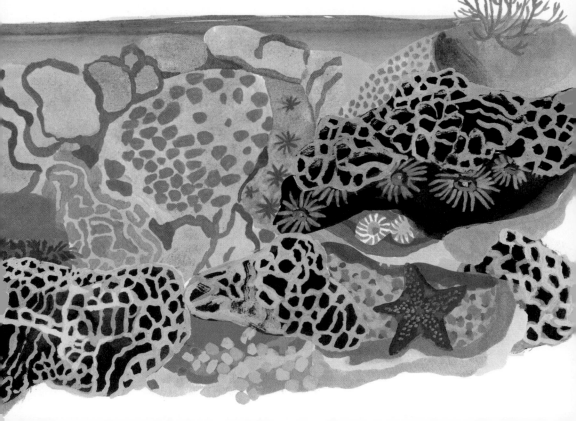

SEA RANCH

From Salt Point State Park, it takes about forty minutes to get to Point Arena. On your way, you'll pass Sea Ranch. Steeped in the idealism of the 1960s, this private community offers gorgeous and exclusive vacation rentals. On the east side of Highway 1, the tiny, nondenominational **Sea Ranch Chapel** is a peaceful place to stop for a moment. It was designed by artist and architect James Hubbell and constructed with local, natural materials.

POINT ARENA

In the mid-1800s, Point Arena served as an important hub of the redwood industry. Today it has a cozy downtown area and an active fishing pier from which local divers head out for abalone. Visit **Bird Café and Supper Club** for seasonal cuisine. Then make your way to **Point Arena Lighthouse** to climb to the top. The tallest lighthouse along the Pacific coast, it was constructed in 1870 but had to be rebuilt in 1908 after it was leveled by the 1906 San Francisco earthquake. Visit the museum on the ground floor to learn more about the lighthouse's history.

MENDOCINO

It's about an hour of desolate coastal road from Point Arena to Mendocino. Overlooking the Pacific Ocean atop rugged cliffs, surrounded by a state park, Mendocino is a laid-back, artsy town with charming historic homes and water towers sprinkled throughout. Historically, they were accompanied by a windmill, which would power water up to the tank. Many towers have been converted to living quarters and even hotel rooms. Stroll along Main Street and find the bookstore, the **Ford House Museum**, the toy shop, the chocolatier, B and Bs, cafés, and restaurants. A few blocks away toward the ocean, you'll see the wildflowers and scrub that make up the edge of **Mendocino Headlands State Park**. Starting at Church Street, the **Mendocino Headlands Trail** is 4 miles out and back.

Point Cabrillo Light Station

Just five minutes north of Mendocino is Point Cabrillo Light Station. Park and walk, either on the paved road or the more rugged trail, to this working lighthouse and its restored outbuildings. The top floor, with the original Fresnel lens, is open for viewing just a handful of days a year, but you can visit the **Light Station Museum** year-round. If you visit between November and May, you might get lucky and spot migrating whales offshore.

FORT BRAGG

As you roll into Mendocino County's biggest coastal city, stop at **Mendocino Coast Botanical Gardens**, where the garden extends from the highway to the ocean. Fort Bragg is perhaps best known for **Glass Beach**. In the early 1900s, the place was a dump where locals pushed everything from bottles to car parts off the cliffs, but eventually the glass broke down and created a beautiful seashore of tiny pieces of color. Unfortunately, visitors didn't heed the rules restricting glass collection, and nowadays the sea glass is greatly diminished. But at the **Sea Glass Museum**, you can see what the beach once held and learn more about the history of this unique spot.

Abalone, sea glass, rocks, and shells on the beaches of Fort Bragg

DRIVE-THRU TREE

From Fort Bragg, cut inland at Hardy, weaving into the forest to meet Highway 101 at Leggett. (It's beautiful here but an incredibly windy hour and twenty minutes on the road, so if you or your passengers are prone to carsickness, be forewarned.) Just before Leggett, stop at the Drive-Thru Tree, also known as the Chandelier Tree, to begin your journey into the Humboldt Redwoods State Park. The 2,000-year-old tree was carved out in 1937 and is still alive, proof of the redwoods' remarkable ability to heal around their wounds. There's a small fee per car to squeeze through.

HUMBOLDT REDWOODS STATE PARK

In the early 1900s, Save the Redwoods League worked tirelessly to protect the forest from encroaching logging interests, resulting in this park, which today covers 53,000 acres, almost twice the size of San Francisco. About one-third of the park is old growth. Throughout the park, there are more than a hundred miles of trails and many options for a short nature walk. Try the **Rockefeller Loop** or the **Drury-Chaney Loop**. There's also a string of gorgeous campgrounds if you want to spend the night.

The Avenue of the Giants is the scenic road, which runs alongside Highway 101. This slower road runs into the park, taking you through the verdant tunnel of redwoods. This route adds at least two hours to your overall drive, but don't pass it by.

EUREKA

About thirty minutes from Humboldt Redwoods State Park, Eureka is the largest coastal town between San Francisco and Portland. Its historic Victorian homes and buildings will transport you back in time. Visit **Clarke Historical Museum** to learn about the local history and browse the Victorian memorabilia and Native American artifacts. Drive down Hillsdale Street to see the preserved Queen Anne- and Eastlake-style homes dating from the 1880s to the 1920s. On and around 2nd Street, downtown Eureka offers plenty of shopping and dining options. Don't miss **Eureka Books**, a two-floor literary dream come true.

TRINIDAD

A brief trip from Eureka on Highway 101, past Arcata, is this seaside town, perched high on the cliffs. Home to only about 360 residents, it attracts many visitors with its quaintness and amazing views. It's worth renting a home right on the coast and spending a few days here. Sit outside bundled in a blanket to watch the sunset as hummingbirds flit by. After beachcombing on the misty shores in the morning, enjoy a fresh and hearty breakfast in town at **Beachcomber Cafe**. If you'd like to explore a little further, **Trinidad Head Lighthouse Trail** takes you 1.7 miles around Trinidad Harbor and past a sweeping view of the ocean and Trinidad State Beach. At **Humboldt State University Marine Lab**, you can (carefully) caress anemones and urchins in the outdoor touch tanks.

Agate Beach

Part of **Patrick's Point State Park**, this beach lies below the Trinidad bluffs, from which secluded homes enjoy expansive ocean views. The shores hold colorful rocks and milky crystal agates. According to a local rock collector, the most unique rock here is Trinidad jasper, found only on these shores. The entrance at Big Lagoon is the easy, flat way in, but at Patrick's Point, you can hike down and get a panoramic view of the shores.

Trinidad State Beach

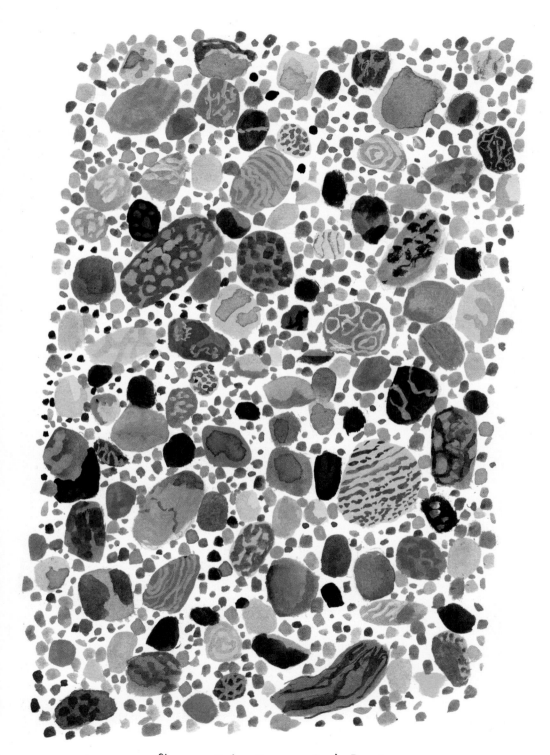

Stones washed ashore on Agate Beach

REDWOOD NATIONAL AND STATE PARKS

This network of four parks encompasses Redwood National Park (created in 1968) and three California State Parks (created in the 1920s): Prairie Creek, Del Norte Coast, and Jedediah Smith. Leave at least a full day to explore them. As you head out of Trinidad and into the Redwood Parks, look for herds of Roosevelt elk (named after their benefactor President Theodore Roosevelt), which have the largest antlers of all elk species; they can be up to 4 feet long. The **Newton B. Drury Scenic Parkway** winds through old-growth forests in Prairie Creek Redwoods State Park and is an easy introduction to the park and all that it has to offer. There are turnoffs and trails throughout the parks; **Lady Bird Johnson Grove Trail**, **Tall Trees Grove Loop Trail**, and the more challenging **Rhododendron Trail** are among the popular ones.

Fern Canyon

Fern Canyon, located in Prairie Creek, takes a bit of work to get to, but its fern- and moss-covered canyon walls are worth it. From Trinidad, take Highway 101 for thirty minutes, turning onto Davison Road and taking that for another thirty minutes. The unpaved road can be a little dodgy, and may be flooded in parts. Once you make it to the incredibly lush canyon, mini waterfalls stream down the 50-foot walls to keep the ferns hydrated. While there are wooden boards to walk on, your feet will still get wet, so stash a clean, dry pair of socks in the car. Back on the road, when making your way to Del Norte Coast Redwoods State Park, keep your eye out for a towering 50-foot-tall Paul Bunyan and his ox, Babe. They are the mascots of the **Trees of Mystery**, a privately owned, quintessential roadside attraction that's a piece of Americana, taking you on a trail past wooden sculptures carved by chain saw and leading to a gondola ride above the treetops.

From the edge of Del Norte Coast Redwoods State Park, it's thirty minutes on Highway 101 to reach Oregon's southern border. If your trip ends here, the nearest airport is in Medford, Oregon, a two-hour drive inland on Route 199.

Rhododendron Trail

Paul and Babe
at the
Trees of Mystery

COMMON NORTHERN CALIFORNIA WILDLIFE

Bobcat

The most common wildcat in North America, the bobcat plays an important role in maintaining healthy ecosystem function by controlling prey populations, including birds, mule deer, and bighorn sheep. It lives in environments with dense vegetative cover or steep rocky terrain.

Alligator Lizard

Active during daylight, the alligator lizard is often found underneath debris and beach driftwood. You might see one zipping across the ground.

California Mountain King Snake

This species is nonvenomous and spends most of its time underground or hidden in brush.

Black-Tailed Deer

One of six subspecies of mule deer in California, the black-tailed deer was first recorded by the Lewis and Clark Expedition—which Thomas Jefferson commissioned in 1804 to study the region's plants, animals, and geography—and can be found up and down the West Coast. It tends to forage at dawn and dusk, an important thing to keep in mind if you are driving during these times.

Scrub Jay

Vocal and inquisitive, the scrub jay can be found in parks, forests, and even urban neighborhoods. When a scrub jay dies, others will gather around it, screeching for up to thirty minutes in a kind of avian funeral.

Turkey Vulture

This long-winged bird is commonly seen around open areas such as roadsides, suburbs, and farm fields—and food sources where it's easy to go in for seconds, such as landfills, trash heaps, and construction sites.

California Quail

Keep your eyes peeled low to the ground if you want to spot a California quail—it is most often seen strutting across clearings. But maintain your distance and stay quiet, because if it notices your presence, it may burst into fast, low flight.

Raccoon

Raccoons are nocturnal but can occasionally be seen during daylight hours, and these scavengers will certainly get into your food if it's left out overnight.

CHAPTER 3

Oregon

Welcome to
OREGON

While California is defined by long stretches of smooth, sandy beaches, Oregon is known for its rugged, harsh coastline. Forty-one percent of this dramatic coastline is made up of rocky shores composed of tide pools, headlands, and cliffs. This border between land and sea is part of a vibrant ecosystem, one that's beautiful to explore but essential to respect and protect.

As you travel north along the Pacific Coast Highway, the dense trees of Redwood National Park start to break up, offering glimpses of the shore again when you enter Oregon. Highway 101 joins the coast, winding along the Samuel H. Boardman State Scenic Corridor, offering plenty of spots to stop and admire the view. Rolling grassy hills dramatically fall into the ocean, where giant sea stacks stick out like errant teeth.

The Oregon coastline can be rough and windy, its cliffs and beaches sculpted by time and the raging waters of the Pacific, all of it surrounded by a dense fog. But just around the corner, conditions can change in an instant. The fog lifts to reveal a long sandy beach, golden dunes melting into the dark green forest, where the sun illuminates the ferns and undergrowth below.

Perilous conditions make the waters incredibly difficult to navigate, and lighthouses dot the headlands all along the coast, beacons for those at sea. Misty trails through ancient pine forests wind past gentle streams, offering a contrast to the harsher beaches. This distinct coastline is an intersection of pastoral and rugged, the kind of place to wear a floral prairie dress with your hiking boots. A place where you can embark on a new adventure at any given moment.

Oregon's coast and landscape are untamed and majestic with many nooks within which to find solitude. Walking around an Oregon beach is like being on your own scavenger hunt, looking for a cluster of starfish or a sparkly agate. Other times it feels like an obstacle course; hop past algae, don't tread on the barnacles, sidestep that pool, then scurry over a bunch of driftwood to reach the shore.

The most populated area on the coast is in North Bend/Coos Bay, which has only around 26,000 residents. Small towns make for cozy, welcoming communities where you can find fresh seafood and snug cafés. Some are fishing towns with active harbors, like Garibaldi and Newport. The shops are just as fun to hop around as the beaches. An antiques mall or bookstore can be the perfect place to warm up after a brisk beach adventure.

Every year, no matter the season, people flock to the Oregon coast, whether it's for whale watching in Depoe Bay, to see some of the 18,000 gray whales that migrate past; thrill seeking in the Oregon Dunes National Recreation Area; or eating freshly caught seafood, like razor clams and crab, on the beach in front of a campfire.

Traversed by elaborate bridges that reach into the sky, rivers like the Rogue and the Umpqua spit out into the Pacific. While the coastline, with its sea stacks and headlands, is stunning, the forests along the Oregon coast are as notable as the beaches. In Oswald West State Park, trails take you through old-growth Sitka spruce and Douglas fir trees; rusty brown ground coverings, soft with decomposing needles, help new life thrive. The forests are dewy with coastal mist, a refreshing atmosphere for a hike. From lookouts and viewpoints, you can see islands and sea stacks peeking out of the water. All the offshore rocks and islands in Oregon are protected wildlife refuges, and they welcome a diversity of birds and marine life that have stories of their own.

If you can, spend some time camping in one of the many state parks and campgrounds along the Oregon coast. There's no better way to experience this landscape firsthand, unzipping your tent to the morning sun, taking in the cool air and crisp smell of pine.

Our next adventure is just ahead.

BROOKINGS → ASTORIA
338 miles
7.5 hours (without stops)
5-8 days

Destinations

Natural Bridges

BROOKINGS

Just a few miles north of the California border, Oregon's southernmost coastal town welcomes you with its remarkably pretty beaches and forests. Established in the early 1900s by John E. Brookings, a timber baron who wanted to expand lumber production to the southern Oregon coast, in the 1920s, Brookings became a center for growing Easter lily bulbs, an industry that is still thriving today. Directly north of town, **Harris Beach State Park** offers great overnight camping among conifers and wildflowers. The campsites are a short walk from the shores, where you can meander around sea stacks and beachcomb at low tide. Stay for a surreal pastel sunset that's fit for a fairy tale.

Samuel H. Boardman State Scenic Corridor

The entire Oregon coast is a scenic byway, but between Brookings and Port Orford, the Samuel H. Boardman State Scenic Corridor features a particular density of turnoffs to explore hikes and viewpoints. Thick fog can often cloud the coastline, but the moody environs are quite beautiful too. **Natural Bridges** is one of many scenic pullouts right off Highway 101. A short five- to ten-minute hike through brush, flowers, and wild mushrooms is rewarded with a view of several natural bridge formations.

GUIDE TO BEACHCOMBING

Beaches change yearly, daily, hourly. Look closely, and incremental changes can even be seen in the tiny instant of a second, with sand, rocks, and water constantly shifting—you never know what you're going to find. Here are a few things to take into consideration when beachcombing.

- **CHECK THAT BEACHCOMBING IS PERMITTED.** Most beaches on the coast allow you to take a few items as souvenirs; however, there are beaches that strictly prohibit collecting, particularly "marine gardens" and their adjacent beaches. Always look out for signs by the parking lot.

- **BRING SOMETHING TO COLLECT IN.** Pack a bunch of resealable plastic bags or containers and a permanent marker. Write down the beach's name and the date so you remember where your rocks came from.

- **COLLECT RESPONSIBLY.** Don't leave the beach with buckets of rocks; just take a few of your favorites so there are plenty left for the next people to discover.

- **CHECK LOCAL TIDE TABLES.** The best time for beachcombing is two hours after a high tide. The shore will be ripe with freshly exposed sea treasures.

What to Look For

- **AGATES.** These stones with pretty striations almost look like they're glowing. Look for them in creeks crossing the beach or gravel beds. They are easiest to find when they're wet.

- **PETRIFIED WOOD AND FOSSILS.** Storm action tosses up the rock beds and exposes areas that have been buried for millions of years. Anything with grains or lines or a shell impression is worth a second look.

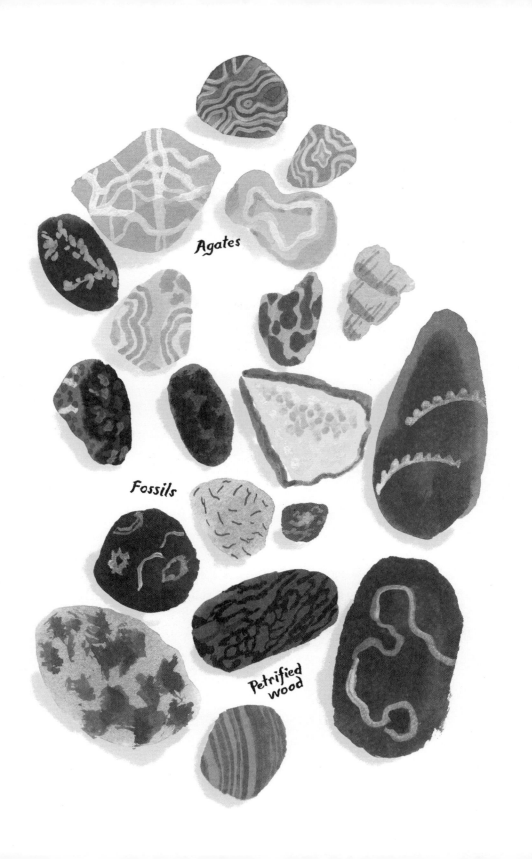

Agates

Fossils

Petrified wood

GOLD BEACH

In this small coastal town, about thirty-five minutes north of Brookings, the Rogue River meets the Pacific Ocean, with a grandiose bridge that's also a National Historic Civil Engineering Landmark. Refuel and charge up with a coffee while browsing two floors of used books at **Gold Beach Books**. With more than 75,000 used and new books in stock, it's the largest bookstore on the Oregon coast.

PORT ORFORD

Port Orford, a small fishing town with an artistic bent, is thirty-five minutes north of Gold Beach. The oldest town on the Oregon Coast, it's also the most westerly in the contiguous United States. South of town, at **Humbug Mountain State Park**, you can hike through the forested hills, spotting maples and Oregon myrtle, and then stroll along the beach. As you roll into town, stop at **Battle Rock Park** for a view out to the Redfish Rocks Marine Reserve. In town, the **Hawthorne Gallery** displays a wide variety of abstract and contemporary art. Many of the thirty artists are local, and ten are members of the Hawthorne family. Stop at the family's restaurant, **Redfish**, next door to dine and take in a view of the coast. A few miles north of Port Orford, turn off Highway 101 for a short detour to **Cape Blanco State Park**, which marks Oregon's westernmost point. Within the park, overlooking the Pacific, sits the **Cape Blanco Lighthouse**, Oregon's oldest.

Battle Rock Park

OREGON LIGHTHOUSES

Oregon's coastal lighthouses are a piece of maritime history. The state's first lighthouse was built on the mouth of the Umpqua River, its inaugural lighting in 1857. Seven years later, Umpqua River Lighthouse collapsed into its namesake river. Eventually it was rebuilt, along with many others on the coast. Eleven lighthouses remain today.

Pelican Bay
BROOKINGS

Cape Blanco
PORT ORFORD

Coquille River
BANDON

Cape Arago
COOS BAY

Umpqua River
WINCHESTER BAY

Heceta Head
FLORENCE

Cleft of the Rock CAPE PERPETUA

Yaquina Head
NEWPORT

Yaquina Bay
NEWPORT

Cape Meares
TILLAMOOK

Tillamook Rock TILLAMOOK

BANDON

From Port Orford, Highway 101 leaves the coast for a stretch, taking you through forested mountains. This section is a center of timber industry, and you'll share the road with massive logging trucks. Take a thirty-minute detour off the main highway, toward the coast, and you'll find **Floras Lake**, where you can watch kiteboarders and windsurfers.

Back on Highway 101, in the tiny town of Langlois, fill up your gas tank at the **Langlois Market**, and pick up some craft beer; its selection rivals what you would find in any big-city store. You'll soon come to the shores of Bandon, an ideal place to spend the night and take a rest from the road. Campsites at **Bullards Beach State Park**, just north of the town center, are an easy walk from the ocean. Bandon also has plenty of coastal home rentals if you'd like to be indoors. Bandon's picturesque downtown is lined with shops and fresh seafood restaurants, like **Tony's Crab Shack**; stop in at **Face Rock Creamery** for handmade cheese and ice cream. Check out the **Washed Ashore Gallery**, a nonprofit endeavor that exhibits art made from plastic pollution. Bandon's beaches are recognizable by the elegant sea stacks and boulders along the sandy shore. Go for a long walk and search for agates and sea caves at **Bandon State Natural Area**. Local artist Denny Dyke draws walkable labyrinths in the sand here every day after the tide has gone out.

BANDON'S CRANBERRIES

The mild, wet climate in Bandon, known as the Cranberry Capital of Oregon, is perfect for growing the tart red berries. In September, come for the Bandon Cranberry Festival, where the Cranberry Queen is crowned and locals compete with their favorite cranberry recipes.

Bandon State Natural Area

COOS BAY

Past marshes, dense forests, and the Coquille River, Coos Bay is thirty minutes up Highway 101 from Bandon. Both Coos Bay and the adjacent city of North Bend are home to a bustling port, known for the huge volume of lumber once exported around the world, which helped to make the region a hub for the southern Oregon coast. The **Coos History Museum** can brief you on the area's fishing and logging industries and the Coquille indigenous people. For another reason to stop and stretch your legs, wander the antiques stores in downtown Coos Bay and North Bend.

Antiques at the local thrift store

BOWLINE
KNOT

FIGURE
EIGHT
KNOT

ANGLER'S
LOOP

HALTER
HITCH

On display at the Coos History Museum

Shore Acres State Park

Accessed via a scenic detour from Highway 101 along Cape Arago Highway, this park is 13 miles southwest of downtown Coos Bay. The former estate of timber baron Louis J. Simpson, it is known for its perennials from around the world, on glorious display in a Japanese garden and two rose gardens. For beach access, take the trail down to the secluded cove at **Simpson Beach** or stop at **Sunset Beach** along Cape Arago Highway.

Conde B. McCullough Memorial Bridge

OREGON BRIDGES

The Oregon coastline is transected by a variety of rivers, estuaries, and rocky headlands. In the early twentieth century, this geography meant that many small villages and outposts were incredibly difficult to access. After World War I, Oregon set out to build a highway that would run the entire coastline, what is today US Highway 101. To do so involved a massive effort of bridge building. Many of Oregon's coast bridges were constructed under the leadership of one man: Conde B. McCullough, the state bridge engineer from 1919 to 1935. McCullough's bridges are rich in architectural detail, often embellished with Classical, Gothic, and Art Deco details. The Conde B. McCullough Memorial Bridge, which spans Coos Bay, was said to be his favorite.

OREGON DUNES NATIONAL RECREATION AREA

Stretching for 54 miles, the gigantic and billowy dunes in the Oregon Dunes National Recreation Area are a nice contrast to the craggy rocks of most of coastal Pacific Northwest. There are several outcrops off the road that lead to areas where you can explore the dunes. Made from sedimentary rock uplifted from the Coast Range mountains more than 12 million years ago, and continually shaped by wind and water, these dunes are special: This is one of the largest sections of temperate coastal sand dunes in the world, and supports a diverse ecosystem of flora and fauna. Visit the dunes in the early morning—there's no shade, and climbing up and down in the sand is taxing. You can rent a sand sled, sand board, or dune buggy and ride the dunes like a local. Stop in at the Oregon Dunes Visitor Center in Reedsport for more information.

FLORENCE

Situated alongside the coastal dunes, at the mouth of the Siuslaw River, Florence is a small riverfront town that serves as an access point to the Oregon Dunes and the coast for visitors coming from the inland college town of Eugene. North of town, near Heceta Head, are the **Sea Lion Caves**. If you're looking for a treat in Florence, I recommend the buttermilk donut at **Big Dog Donuts**. Just a few minutes farther on Highway 101 is the **Darlingtonia State Natural Site**, a protected wildlife bog where a unique carnivorous pitcher plant grows. With high hollow tubes that trap insects, the *Darlingtonia californica*, also called the cobra lily, is the only pitcher plant in Oregon. The turnoff from Highway 101 is easy to miss, so be aware.

CAPE PERPETUA

Around 18 miles north of Florence is Cape Perpetua. Here the rugged, craggy basalt shores continue, jutting out into the Pacific. The **Cape Perpetua Headland** is the highest viewpoint accessible by car on the Oregon Coast, and there are many wooded trails to wander through on foot. From the Cape Perpetua Visitor Center, hike the **Captain Cook Trail** down to the rocky waters, tide pools, and **Cook's Chasm**, an aquatic canyon. Here you'll find **Thor's Well**, also known as the "drainpipe of the Pacific," a gaping hole in the rocks that sucks ocean water in, then sprays it out. The waves at Cape Perpetua are most dramatic at high tide, and really exciting to experience. But be mindful: Never turn your back on the water, as unexpectedly large waves can sneak up and pull you out to sea.

Thor's Well

Crashing waves at Cook's Chasm

Moonflowers in Yachats

YACHATS

Five minutes north of Cape Perpetua is Yachats. Nicknamed the "Gem of the Oregon Coast," this quirky small town—pronounced Yah-Hots—is an ideal place to stay for a few nights. It's breathtakingly beautiful, and there's a range of hikes, from low-key forest trails to cliffside climbs. Its **804 Trail** starts at the Smelt Sands Recreation Site and runs along the western edge of town, connecting to a 7-mile stretch of sandy beach north of town where you can search for agates. Grab pastries at **Bread & Roses Bakery** or breakfast from **Green Salmon Coffee Company**.

NEWPORT

Thirty-five minutes north of Yachats is Newport, a fishing town and popular tourist destination. Before crossing the Yaquina Bay into Newport, stop in South Beach to visit Oregon's famous **Rogue Brewery** as well as the **Oregon Coast Aquarium**, where you can learn about some of the state's native marine life up close. Once in Newport, walk down to the bayfront, and try to follow the boisterous barks to **Sea Lion Docks**. The sea lions are a very vocal group! Lining the bayfront here are restaurants like **Sharks Seafood Bar & Steamer Co.** On Newport's ocean shore, **Nye Beach** is the charming Old Town with shops, restaurants, and the **Sylvia Beach Hotel**, named for American bookseller and publisher Sylvia Beach, who opened the Shakespeare and Company bookstore in Paris in 1919. You can stay in one of the author-themed rooms; choose among J. K. Rowling, F. Scott Fitzgerald, Mark Twain, Colette, and more. There's no TV or Wi-Fi, just books and tranquility.

The Sylvia Beach Hotel

Yaquina Head Outstanding Natural Area

Since 1873, the lighthouse at Yaquina Head has been guiding ships, and at 93 feet, it's Oregon's tallest. Visit the lighthouse, and investigate the nearby tide pools and **Cobble Beach**, where the shore is made up of black basalt stones dating back to a lava flow 14 million years ago. Listen for the sound of the stones rattling when the tide comes in. An array of wildlife calls this area home, and if you're lucky, you may spot hordes of migratory birds, like murres and pelicans, and maybe even breaching whales.

OTTER ROCK

A brief trip from Yaquina Head, Otter Rock—named after the rocky off-shore island that was a former hangout for otters—is a tiny town with misty views of hillside houses. Drive straight into town and stop at **Devil's Punchbowl**, where you can watch the surfers, or make your way down to the beach to walk alongside the waves. These days you'd be incredibly lucky to find an otter in Otter Rock. With the densest fur of any mammal, otters are made for the cold waters of the Pacific. But the dense and glossy fur that protected them in their home environment also made them a prime target of the fur trade. Sadly, sea otters were hunted to near extinction during the eighteenth and nineteenth centuries. Washington and California have managed to reintroduce otter populations, but Oregon has struggled. There is now a renewed interest among scientists and activists to bring this once-native species back. Until they succeed, you can find otters at the Oregon Coast Aquarium in Newport.

For a quiet detour along the town's coastline, pass Otter Rock on Highway 101 and turn onto the Otter Crest Loop, a one-way southbound road accessible just south of Depoe Bay, winding along the cliffs with stunning views the whole way.

The beach at Devil's Punchbowl

DEPOE BAY

Called the "Whale Watching Capital of the Oregon Coast," this bright and colorful town is the place to see these majestic mammals. Visit the **Whale Watching Center** or the nearby **Boiler Bay State Scenic Viewpoint** to try to spot them from the shore. Or take a whale tour on the water, led by a marine biologist. The best times to come are in December and March, when there are specific whale watching weeks during migration periods as 20,000 gray whales head from their breeding waters in Mexico to Alaska. The food source is rich in the waters near Depoe Bay, so chances are good that you'll spot one here. On your way out of Depoe Bay, stop at **Fogarty Creek State Recreation Area**, for hiking trails and beach access.

Whale watching in Depoe Bay

LINCOLN CITY

Continue twenty minutes north on Highway 101 to Lincoln City. On the 45th parallel, halfway between the equator and the North Pole, Lincoln City is a popular summer tourist destination for Oregon travelers. The coastal winds make it a hot spot for kite flying, particularly during the annual Kite Festivals in June and October. In town, browse the **Little Antique Mall**, brimming with coastal antiques, basketry, beaded purses, and ceramics. At **Time Capsule Antiques & More**, you'll find a unique assortment from books to Bakelite, and friendly owners who gift patrons with local agates.

From Lincoln City, take an optional detour off Highway 101 onto Brooten Road to Pacific City. It's easy to recognize Pacific City's Haystack Rock (Cannon Beach farther north has its own Haystack Rock), which rises 327 feet out of the water at Cape Kiwanda State Natural Area.

TILLAMOOK

From Pacific City, drive thirty-five minutes inland on OR-131 to Tillamook. This part of Oregon is dairy country. Take a tour of **Tillamook Creamery** (also known as "the cheese factory") and treat yourself to its ice cream or cheese for a beachside picnic (see tips on making an excellent cheese board opposite). **Blue Heron French Cheese Company**, a smaller cheesemaker, is worth a visit for its café, wine tastings, cheese shop (including its specialty, Brie), and petting zoo.

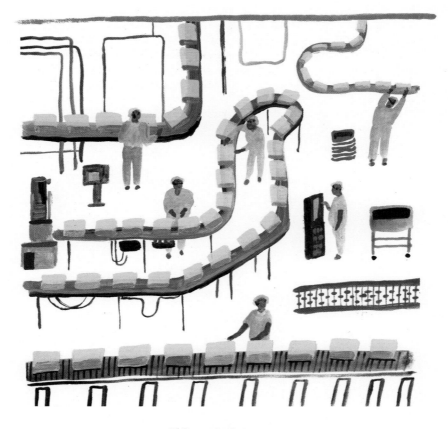

Tillamook Creamery

THE ESSENTIALS OF
AN EXQUISITE CHEESE PLATE

Even for a beach picnic, there's no reason to skimp on a good cheese board. With plenty of dairy farms in the region, there are lots of local options. Below are some suggestions for cheese and what to serve with them. Add a side salad to make a meal out of it.

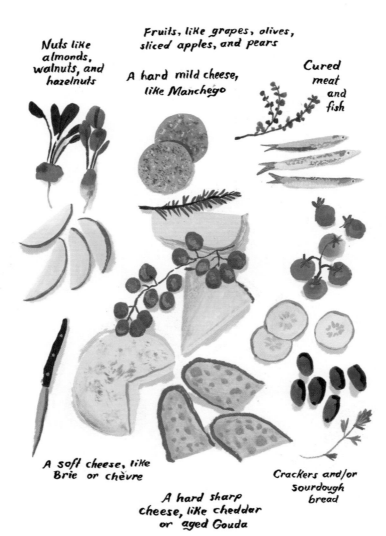

Nuts like almonds, walnuts, and hazelnuts

Fruits, like grapes, olives, sliced apples, and pears

A hard mild cheese, like Manchego

Cured meat and fish

A soft cheese, like Brie or chèvre

A hard sharp cheese, like cheddar or aged Gouda

Crackers and/or sourdough bread

GARIBALDI

The quiet fishing town of Garibaldi, located at the northern end of Tillamook Bay, is the perfect place to stop for seafood. Stretch your legs on a walk around the marina docks, where fishing and leisure boats come and go all day. At the **Myrtlewood Factory** in town, sort through all kinds of wooden objects made from local myrtle trees, which the store calls "nature's gift to Oregon."

MYRTLE

Also known as California bay laurel or pepperwood, Oregon myrtle grows more than 90 feet tall and is found only on the West Coast. Native Americans used its leaves to treat everything from menstrual cramps to headaches. Today it's a beloved medium for woodworkers. The heavy wood has a fine grain and intricate patterns, found in the burls, and it's often used for decorative furniture; string instruments, like guitars; and smaller items, like spoons, bowls, and vases.

ROCKAWAY BEACH

It's a quick drive from Garibaldi to Rockaway Beach, where the establishments are spread out along Highway 101. You'll pass purveyors of seafood, pizza, coffee, and ice cream, and shops carrying beach toys and souvenirs. There is easy parking, and once you're on the beach, you'll see a faraway rock formation that looks like it was planted in the sea.

OSWALD WEST STATE PARK

On your way toward Cannon Beach, stop at Oswald West State Park, which is about twenty minutes from Rockaway Beach. The **Cape Falcon Trail** starts out in ferns and dense forest, then opens up to a beautiful view of the beach below. The trail continues alongside the coast and through thick hedges and eventually brings you to the cliffs for an impressive panorama. If you want to see Oregon surfers at their best, opt for the easier **Short Sands Trail**. Both trails are well-trafficked, so start out early.

Cape Falcon Trail →

CANNON BEACH

From Oswald West State Park, it takes ten minutes to get to Cannon Beach. With cottages lining the coast on wooded hillsides, it's perfect for a stroll or a leisurely lunch. Look to the ocean and you'll see **Haystack Rock**, one of two Oregon natural landmarks by this name (see page 153) and a popular landing spot for all kinds of birds, especially tufted puffins. Fans of *The Goonies* may recognize the landscape—much of the cult classic was shot here (and in nearby Astoria; see page 166). An easy drive from Portland, this is a popular destination, particularly on weekends. (Parking is limited, so take the first spot you see.) If you stay overnight, treat yourself to an ocean-front room at an inn or bed-and-breakfast. The next morning, choose a trail to hike at **Ecola State Park**, winding through mossy pines and berry bushes toward the sound of the ocean.

BIRDS OF HAYSTACK ROCK

Rising 235 feet out of the water, Haystack is protected as part of the Oregon Islands National Wildlife Refuge and a habitat for diverse bird life. Here are some of the species you may spot.

Common murre

Tufted puffin

Brandt's cormorant

Pigeon guillemot

Rhinoceros auklet

Western gull

Sanderling

Brown pelican

Black oystercatcher

PORTLAND

While not directly on the coastal route, Portland is worth a less-than-two-hour detour. You can easily drive east from Cannon Beach, Tillamook, or Astoria, their highways taking you across the Oregon Coast range and dropping you into Portland. Portland has always had a reputation for being a little eccentric, as the bumper stickers "Keep Portland Weird" will tell you (the phrase was borrowed from Austin). Today it has become a dynamic hub of business, food, and outdoor life, with residents who appreciate a city that puts an emphasis on sustainability and living well. Bicycles abound, and a light rail system makes getting around simple. There are award-winning restaurants and access to fresh, local food at the city's many farmers' markets. For book lovers, the crown jewel is **Powell's City of Books**. Covering an entire city block, it holds more than a million titles and a café, so you can spend hours here. See why Portland is called the City of Roses at one of the nearby gardens: the **International Rose Test Garden**, the **Japanese Garden**, or the **Lan Su Chinese Garden** downtown. If you want to hike, **Forest Park** in Northwest Portland offers more than 80 miles of trails. Its 5,200 acres make it one of the largest urban forests in the United States. After all that fresh air, it's time to caffeinate at one of Portland's homegrown specialty coffee chains, like **Stumptown**, **Heart**, or **Coava**.

Powell's City of Books

Cruising through Portland's neighborhoods

MORE TO SEE IN PORTLAND

The Hoyt Arboretum · Oaks Park Roller Skating Rink · the Oregon Museum of Science and Industry · the Pittock Mansion · the Portland Art Museum · Portland Mercado

OREGON'S LOVE OF COFFEE

Coffee's popularity in the Pacific Northwest might be due to the gray, damp weather that the region endures most of the year. In 1971, Starbucks opened in Seattle, forever changing the coffee industry. Dutch Bros., which started in Grants Pass, Oregon, spent its early years serving coffee from pushcarts before becoming a larger drive-through chain, and Portland is said to have had the first drive-through coffeehouse in the world, originally called Motor Moka. On the road all through the state, you'll see lots of little drive-through espresso huts. One thing is for sure: In this part of the country, people like their coffee, and a lot of it.

FORT CLATSOP

Back on the coastal route, a fifteen-minute drive out of the small city of Astoria will take you to Fort Clatsop, named for the small Native American tribe who lived here. Learn about the Lewis and Clark Expedition—they spent their last winter here. Experience life on the fort by roaming its living quarters. The structures were reconstructed using original notes and drawings. You can also explore the surrounding forests and walk one of the many historic trails used by both the Clatsop and the expedition.

ASTORIA

Astoria is a historic portside city built on the Columbia River that finds a balance between pretty and gritty. It was once known for its fur trading, fishing, and cannery industries and is now a culinary destination. Visit **Fort George Brewery** for locally brewed craft beer. The old-timey downtown is sprinkled with antiques shops, used-book stores, and restaurants. The **Flavel House Museum** was once the home of Captain George Flavel, a bar pilot who helped guide ships through the hazardous waters of the mouth of the Columbia. Admire the ornate woodwork, unique fireplace mantels, antiques, and grand parlors of the Victorian house, which has been restored to its original state. Make your way to the riverwalk that leads you through town along the mighty Columbia, where you can see cargo ships and massive boats navigating the water. At the east end of town on Pier 39, visit the **Hanthorn Cannery Museum**, a time capsule of the city's once bustling Bumble Bee canning factory.

Astoria–Megler Bridge

Pulling out of Astoria to continue north into Washington, you'll drive over the mouth of the Columbia River on the massive 4.1-mile-long Astoria-Megler Bridge. Constructed in 1966, the bridge was made to withstand both extreme weather conditions and the turbulent waters of this area. Since

The Flavel House Museum

Downtown Astoria

Astoria is built on a hill, the Oregon side of this bridge seems sky-high, and if you're scared of heights (like I am), driving across it may be a challenge. Just keep your hands on the wheel and your eyes on the road, and you'll be over the bridge in no time.

If your trip ends in Astoria, Portland international Airport is about two hours away. Take US-30 all the way for a more scenic route, or connect to I-5 for the quickest one.

CHAPTER 4

Washington

Welcome to
WASHINGTON

If the Oregon coast is rugged, then Washington is its unruly and untamed cousin, its geographies and contours similar in look and feel, yet a little rougher around the edges. As you cross over the mighty Columbia River from Astoria, the landscape is all-consuming—thick forests meet rocky and turbulent waters. Quaint beach towns are replaced with trailheads deep in the forest and rustic lodges with smoke trailing from chimneys. While the popular towns of Long Beach and Ocean Shores attract plenty of beachgoers and vacationers, much of this region is dominated by Olympic National Park—Highway 101 encircles it. You'll drive long stretches of desolate road, seeing maybe only a few cars every hour. Cruise control was made for straight and empty roads like these. In much of Washington State, Highway 101 runs inland, so it won't offer the sweeping coastal views of regions farther south. In order to enjoy the coast here, veer off Highway 101 onto smaller state routes.

The northern beaches of Washington are rugged, with shores of pebbles and large stones. Tree-sized driftwood logs, evidence of the harsh storm activity, pile up on beaches like used matchsticks. The craggy rocks in the tidal zones make cozy homes for colorful anemones and starfish. Within the dense coastal forests, the misty atmosphere in this part of Washington sustains life for hundreds of plant species. Prehistoric-looking ferns cover the floor of old-growth forests where tree limbs are draped with moss. What you've heard about the persistent rain in Washington is true: This region gets more rain than anywhere else in the contiguous United States.

The indigenous people who lived here thousands of years ago made good use of the abundant natural resources, like red cedar, for building canoes and homes. The Quinault and the Makah are among twenty-nine federally recognized tribes in Washington who are still united and working to preserve their traditions and land. At the northwesternmost point of the United States, on the Makah Reservation, is Cape Flattery. Looking out across the Salish Sea, you can see Vancouver Island in the distance. Crossing the sea to get there is actually easy (with a passport); Victoria's port is accessible off Highway 101 by way of ferry from Port Angeles.

The colorful quirky towns that dot the coastal regions of Vancouver Island are one reason this is an extremely popular place for tourists, especially in the summer months. People come here for the farm-to-table restaurants, cozy accommodations, and outdoor adventures of all kinds. Thanks to an inherent respect for nature on the part of those who live here, much of Vancouver Island has been untouched, particularly in its more desolate northern part. A nature lover's paradise, the island offers an endless number of hiking trails to explore. You can easily add five to seven days to your overall journey.

Back on US soil, Highway 101 takes you east past lavender fields and farms, through Bainbridge Island, onto another ferry, which drops you off in Seattle. This hilly city that sits on the southern shores of Puget Sound is known for its relaxed, outdoorsy vibe. With so much incredible nature surrounding the city—you can see glimpses of Mount Rainier, which is 14,417 feet high and 85 miles southeast—it's plain to see why Seattle has been a proponent of a zero-waste lifestyle, making efforts to implement a culture of sustainability. It's a city of neighborhoods, each with its own charm and burgeoning food scene. No matter where you are, you won't be hard pressed to find a coffee shop here; the gray, damp weather is just the setting for a piping hot cup of joe. Zip up your rain slickers (because only tourists use umbrellas) and in the famous words of Oscar the Grouch, "don't let the sunshine spoil your rain."

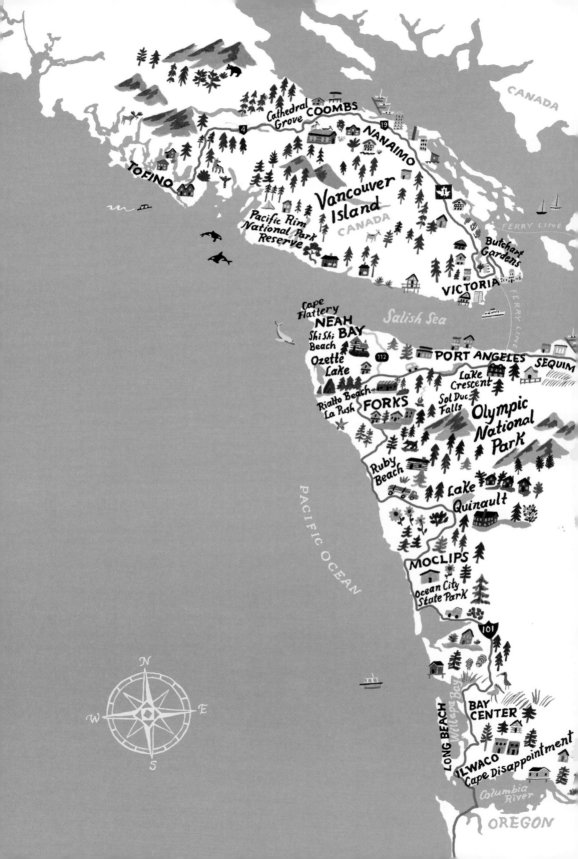

ILWACO → SEATTLE
451 miles
11 hours (without stops)
4-8 days

VICTORIA ↶↷ TOFINO
406 miles
9 hours (without stops)
4-8 days

Destinations

CAPE DISAPPOINTMENT

From the Astoria-Megler Bridge (see page 166), continue onto Highway 101 until you get to Ilwaco. Turn down WA-100 to Cape Disappointment, a large state park with hiking trails, flora, fauna, and ocean vistas. In 1788, British explorer John Meares thought he had found the mouth to the Columbia River, only to realize that it was in fact a bay. His disappointment is reflected in the name he chose for the cape (and for the bay, which he dubbed Deception Bay). The park has played an important role in the region's history. There are two lighthouses in the park: North Head and Cape Disappointment, which is still active and overlooks the waters where the Columbia River meets the Pacific Ocean, a dangerous passage often referred to as the Graveyard of the Pacific. Artist and architect Maya Lin chose Cape Disappointment for one of the sites of her **Confluence Project**; walk along her boardwalk while learning about the Lewis and Clark Expedition. Park campgrounds and yurts are available for overnight stays. From here, it's a short walk to the beach—a great one for kids, who will love to discover what washes ashore, like bull kelp.

North Head Lighthouse

BULL KELP

Kelp are large seaweeds and come in many varieties. Washington is home to some of the most diverse kelp flora in the world, an important part of the local ecosystem. Bull kelp is the area's most common. Underwater, kelp grows in beautiful forests and can reach almost 100 feet, its leaf-like blades soaking in sunlight and nutrients. In the winter, it dies off and floats to the shores.

LONG BEACH

Long Beach and the surrounding area on the Long Beach Peninsula—including the towns of **Seaview** and **Ilwaco**—is a great little hub for antiquing. The **North Coast Antique Mall** is a standout. Downtown Long Beach offers lots of beach town staples like mini golf; stores selling kites, seashells, and oddities, like the mummified "alligator man" at **Marsh's Free Museum**'s gift shop (he's not for sale, but the shop sells other souvenirs); and, of course, beach food: fried fish, funnel cakes, fudge, ice cream, and saltwater taffy. End the day at the Long Beach boardwalk, a suspended pathway through the dunes, and take in the sunset. You can also extend your walk by joining up with the **Discovery Trail**, which you can follow all the way back to Ilwaco.

Maritime antiques at the North Coast Antique Mall

WILLAPA BAY

Back on the coastal highway, the road hugs Willapa Bay, winding through wetlands, estuaries, and coniferous forests, an abundant ecosystem that can be explored in the **Willapa Bay National Wildlife Refuge**, established in 1937 by President Franklin Delano Roosevelt. More than 200 species of birds, including plovers, red-throated loons, and bald eagles, migrate here. From the refuge headquarters, hike the **Art Trail**, a wooden boardwalk over the marshland, to learn about the local wildlife through commissioned works of art.

OYSTERS

There are five types of oysters harvested in Washington, including the Olympia, which is native to the state. Willapa Bay is a prime location for oyster production and was the site for Washington State's most popular oyster, the Pacific oyster. Today Pacific oysters are mainly harvested in the southern Puget Sound, but they can still be purchased directly from producers in Willapa Bay. Nearby Oysterville, on the opposite side of the bay, enjoyed a heyday of oyster production in the 1800s, when its bivalves were in high demand from the discerning denizens of San Francisco. These days, it's a slow and sleepy town.

OCEAN SHORES AND POINT BROWN PENINSULA

From Willapa Bay, continue about ninety minutes to Ocean Shores, passing Aberdeen (birthplace of Kurt Cobain, lead singer of Nirvana, and home to **Kurt Cobain Memorial Park**). Cut west off Highway 101 onto WA-109 to the 6-mile-long Point Brown Peninsula. In the 1960s, a group of Seattle investors developed Ocean Shores here, quickly making it one of the state's best-known beach resort communities. Just to the north of town, **Ocean City State Park** stretches along the coastline; book a cozy beachside campsite here or farther north at **Pacific Beach State Park**. Stock up on food in Ocean Shores before driving into the more desolate areas.

Beach trail from the Ocean City State Park campground

Continue north on WA-109 to Moclips, where you can pay a visit to the **Museum of the North Beach** and browse the curated memorabilia for a dose of local history. From here, the **Quinault Cultural Museum** in Taholah is another fifteen minutes north. The area has long been home to local Native American nations, like the Chinook, Chehalis, and Quinault, and at this small museum, you can learn about the Quinault Indian Nation and view an amazing collection of basketry. (You can't drive farther north on the coast here because of the protected Quinault Reservation.) Return to Highway 101 by cutting inland across on the Moclips Highway, a small two-lane road.

Horseback riding at Ocean Shores

Quinault basketry

OLYMPIC
NATIONAL PARK

Olympic National Park masses 73 miles of rugged coastline and is a gorgeous display of the natural landscape that Washington is known for. Spanning nearly 1 million acres on the Olympic Peninsula, it was established as a National Park in 1938 by President Franklin Delano Roosevelt. The park includes four lush and verdant rain forests—Bogachiel, Hoh, Queets, and Quinault, some parts of which accumulate as much as 15 feet of rain per year—and bustles with wildlife like Roosevelt elk, salamanders, and banana slugs. Hundreds of species of mosses and a variety of ferns give the forests their distinct jungle feeling. The Olympic mountain range is a jumble of peaks, the tallest being glacier-capped Mount Olympus, which stands at 7,965 feet. Only highly experienced mountaineers should attempt its ascent. Most of the beaches are accessible only by hike. Within the park boundaries, the Hoh River Valley is home to one of the quietest places in the United States, as determined by acoustic ecologist Gordon Hempton, a testament to how peaceful it is here. There are no lights around the park, so it's a great place to camp and stargaze next to a crackling fire.

CAMPGROUNDS IN OLYMPIC NATIONAL PARK

Fairholme Campground · Falls Creek Campground · Heart O' the Hills · Hoh Campground · Kalaloch Beach Campground · Mora Campground · Ozette Campground

Hall of Mosses, Hoh Rain Forest

Lake Quinault

One of the gateways to Olympic National Park, Lake Quinault is a perfect place to spend a night or two. Located on the west side of the Olympic Mountains is the enchanting Quinault Rain Forest. There are dozens of trail loops here, like the **Hoh River Trail**, alongside cascading waterfalls. The forest is abundant in berries, flowers, and mushrooms, food for a variety of animals and insects. **Lake Quinault Lodge**, built in 1926 and listed on the National Register of Historic Places, is host to a mushroom festival in October each year. Its outdoor deck, overlooking a grassy field and serene lake waters, is the place to relax with a drink.

Lake Quinault Lodge

Ruby Beach

From Lake Quinault, Highway 101 heads west back toward the coast, passing Olympic National Park's only coastal lodging, **Kalaloch Lodge**. The separate **Kalaloch Campground** is known for its picturesque setting overlooking the ocean. About fifteen minutes north of here, Ruby Beach is one of the park's most well-known beaches. It's a magical landscape of stone-filled shores, moss-covered outcroppings, sea stacks, and robust, aged driftwood. Take the pebble path from the parking lot to the beach, and then scramble over driftwood and rocks to reach the shore. Check local tide tables to make sure you arrive when the time is right and the tide is out.

TREES OF OLYMPIC NATIONAL PARK

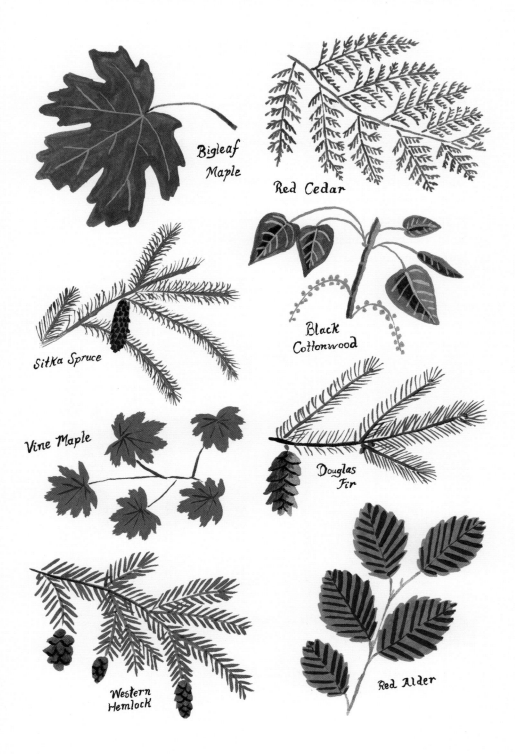

Bigleaf Maple

Red Cedar

Sitka Spruce

Black Cottonwood

Vine Maple

Douglas Fir

Western Hemlock

Red Alder

FORKS

From Ruby Beach, it's about thirty minutes on Highway 101 to the town of Forks, where you'll notice nods to the *Twilight* series, which is based here and in the nearby Hoh Rain Forest. Stop at **John's Beachcombing Museum**, featuring an eccentric collection of objects that have drifted ashore—bottles, buoys, baby dolls, fossils, nets, shells. Drive on WA-110 toward **La Push**, which sits at the mouth of the Quillayute River, and stop at **Second Beach** for a hike, passing through about a mile of old-growth forest, ending on a misty driftwood-strewn beach. If it's low tide, look for critters clinging to the sea stacks.

Japanese tsunami debris at John's Beachcombing Museum

RIALTO BEACH

From Forks, continue for about twenty minutes on WA-110 to Rialto Beach, another famed Olympic National Park Beach. It's not your typical sandy beach—as they are at Ruby Beach, the shores here are pebbly—so wear sneakers or rugged sandals. Walk a mile and a half north to **Hole-in-the-Wall**, a natural arch. When the tide is out, you can explore the tide pools under the arch. At high tide, there is an overland trail to take you over the top. This is a perfect place to catch the sunset, when the sea stacks darken to silhouettes against the colorful sky. **Mora Campground** is up the road if you want to stay the night.

WILD BERRIES

In spring, summer, and fall, forests are peppered with bright berries. Not sure what is edible? Ask a knowledgeable local to help you. Eat only what you can identify with certainty.

SALMONBERRIES. A member of the rose family, salmonberries are similar in size to blackberries but with a bright golden-orange hue. They are one of the first berries to ripen in June/July.

SALAL BERRIES. The bright green leaves of the salal bush are commonly found in floral arrangements, but the dusty, dark-blue berries—ripening toward the end of summer—can also be eaten.

BLACKBERRIES. There are three blackberry varieties found in Washington. The most common, with large, dark purple, plump fruit, is the Himalayan blackberry, originally imported and, because of how quickly it takes over, classified as a noxious weed.

HUCKLEBERRIES. In season from mid-August to mid-September, these dark-blue berries have played an important part in traditional foodways, and today are popular in jam and pies.

THIMBLEBERRIES. Thimbleberries look like small raspberries. Once picked, these tart berries have a hollow shape, hence the name.

NEAH BAY

From Forks, take Highway 101 and a series of state roads to the north-west tip of the Olympic Peninsula, where you'll find Neah Bay, the ancestral home and hub of the Makah people. This hour-long drive brings you through Clallam Bay, Sekiu, and finally onto the Makah Reservation and its **Makah Museum**. From here, a short scenic drive leads to **Cape Flattery**, the northwesternmost point of the continental United States. A magical hike to the beach will take you to emerald-green waters and expansive views of the dramatic cliffs. You'll need a Makah Recreation Pass, which you can pick up at the Makah Museum or at one of the local gas stations. The same pass is valid for Shi Shi Beach (see page 196).

The trail to Cape Flattery

SHI SHI BEACH

From Neah Bay, drive an hour to Shi Shi (pronounced "shy shy") Beach, a true tide pool metropolis and one of Washington's most captivating beaches. Majestic sea stack peaks jut out amid the rough waves. Plan to get here at low tide to be able to fully explore this coastal wilderness. A thirty-minute hike wends through rain forest, the muddy trail covered in ferns. (This is a region with a lot of precipitation, even in the summer.) Most of the trail, and the trailhead, is on the Makah Reservation. Ask for directions; cell service is not reliable, and GPS won't get you there. From the beach, you can opt for a longer hike to **Point of the Arches**, 8 miles round-trip from the Shi Shi Beach parking lot.

The trail down to Shi Shi Beach

OZETTE LAKE

Travelers with a little extra time should consider a day trip or overnight camping at Ozette Lake, about a ninety-minute detour down Hoko Ozette Road from WA-112. In the 1970s, a rough storm along the coast eroded some of the beach near Cape Alava and revealed a perfectly preserved Makah village that had been covered by a mudslide around 1560. Starting at Ozette Lake, hike the 9-mile Cape Alava Loop to see the petroglyphs at **Wedding Rocks**.

Makah petroglyphs etched in a boulder at Wedding Rocks

SOL DUC FALLS

Once you've reconnected with Highway 101, it's 15 miles to Sol Duc Road, which leads you to the falls' trailhead. This lush and mossy trail is about 1.5 miles, taking you into the heart of old-growth forest and to the famed three-pronged cascading falls. At the falls, you'll find a wooden platform, a perfect place to sit and look for rainbows appearing in the cool mist that rises from the crashing water.

LAKE CRESCENT

From Sol Duc Falls, it takes thirty minutes to get to Lake Crescent, a glacially carved lake with waters often still enough for perfectly mirrored reflections of the surrounding trees and ridgelines. On the north shore of the lake, hike along the **Spruce Railroad Trail**, a relatively flat hike spanning 11 miles one way. Closer to the highway, a short hike from the shores of the lake leads you to **Marymere Falls**, a 90-foot-high waterfall. Right across the road, the **Lake Crescent Lodge**, opened in 1915, is a welcoming spot where weary travelers and hikers can enjoy the splendor of the lake or relax in front of the huge stone fireplace.

PORT ANGELES

Drive thirty minutes on Highway 101, past the Elwha River, and arrive in Port Angeles. A hub of the Olympic Peninsula, Port Angeles is a jumping-off point for exploring the northern part of Olympic National Park. Situated directly on the Strait of Juan de Fuca, the small but robust town boasts a prime location where mountains and dense forests gradually ease into the sea. This is an area known for its outdoor adventures, from hiking up **Hurricane Ridge** and mountain biking on the **Olympic Discovery Trail** to exploring the beaches' tidepools. A cluster of restaurants and shops can be found near the **Black Ball Ferry Line Terminal**. Downtown Port Angeles was once the site of a Klallam village called čixʷícən (transliterated as Tse-whit-zen). Discovered in 2003, it is the second-largest Native American village to be found in the state (after the Makah's Ozette village; see page 198), and its artifacts are permanently housed at the **Elwha Klallam Heritage Center**. Stop in at the Olympic National Park Visitor Center for information on visiting the park as well as procuring appropriate permits and maps. Victoria, British Columbia, is only a ferry ride away, providing easy access to Vancouver Island (see page 202).

VANCOUVER ISLAND, CANADA

You'll need your passport to take the one-and-a-half-hour ferry ride from Port Angeles to Victoria on the **Black Ball Ferry Line**, crossing the Strait of Juan de Fuca to Vancouver Island. Much like the coastline in Washington, parts of Vancouver Island feel very remote. Victoria is Vancouver's largest city (and the capital of British Columbia) with about 90,000 people. While the climate is generally mild, the island is the largest on the Pacific coast of North America and therefore has variable weather depending on where you are. The temperatures are warm for Canada, and the western portion of the island is known to be wetter than the east, so bring your rain jacket. The southeastern portion of the island is the most heavily populated, and a great route for road-trip sightseeing. (If you have the time, plan five to seven days to drive the route around the southern portion of the island.) This itinerary is best followed from May to October as the remainder of the year is subject to stormy weather, and many places will be closed.

Northern Vancouver Island is far less developed, an enclave of preserved backcountry home to black bears, wolves, deer, and abundant bird species. To extend your trip, a straight shot about six hours up Highway 19 will land you in **Port Hardy**, the northern terminus of that highway. There's plenty to explore, including **Cape Scott Provincial Park**, situated at the northwest tip of the island, and **Telegraph Cove**, which offers amazing nature viewing offshore, including of humpback whales, dolphins, seals, sea lions, and eagles. No matter where you choose to go, the island provides an endless amount of nature, trails, and quaint seaside towns befitting a Wes Anderson movie.

Cathedral Grove in Nanaimo

Victoria

Immediately off the ferry from Port Angeles, you'll drive into Victoria, one of the oldest cities in the Pacific Northwest. Park your car and wander Victoria's **Inner Harbour** to see the boats and floating homes. Victoria is also known for its European aesthetic, seen in its preserved historic buildings, such as the **Royal British Columbia Museum**; the **Parliament Buildings**; the **Empress Hotel**, a wonderful place for tea; and **Craigdarroch Castle**, built in 1890 by a wealthy couple who at the time were among the richest on the island thanks to the Vancouver Island coal industry. The estate is filled with gorgeous woodwork, antiques, and exquisite stained glass. Walk the coastal trail from Holland Point Park to Clover Point Park, with opportunities to descend to the shore and meander along the water.

High tea at the Empress Hotel

The Butchart Gardens

About thirty minutes outside Victoria, with a boost from the mild coastal climate, the Butchart Gardens present 55 acres of breathtaking, colorful gardens year-round, welcoming more than 1 million visitors annually. The site itself is an old limestone quarry, where in the early 1900s husband and wife Robert and Jennie Butchart built a cement plant. As the limestone deposits became depleted, Jennie had the vision to turn the defunct quarry into a garden, which she named the Sunken Garden.

Nanaimo

From Butchart Gardens, backtrack toward Victoria, then take BC-1 north about ninety minutes to Nanaimo, Vancouver Island's second-largest city and the namesake of the Nanaimo bar, a dessert that even has a trail devoted to it, spanning more than thirty places to get the treat. Nanaimo has played an important role in Vancouver Island's history, once serving as an outpost of the Hudson's Bay Company, originally a fur-trading business and now a retail chain. Whale watching is a top attraction here. Embark on a tour to see humpback whales and orcas, with the added benefit of views of Vancouver Island and the surrounding islands. Near the harbor in the **Old City Quarter**, culinary options abound. Just south of the city, drive the **Cedar Yellow Point Artisan Trail Loop** past farms and artist studios.

Coombs

From Nanaimo, continue on BC-19 for about forty minutes to the small community of Coombs, best known for its "Goats on the Roof"—literally the goats that live atop the **Old Country Market**. Each spring, a herd of goats arrive to make their home on the sod roof and graze on the grass. Used for centuries in northern Scandinavia, green roofs, like the one atop the market, absorb rainwater, insulate, decrease stress, and provide a habitat for wildlife, even goats. From here, start your journey inland on BC-4.

Cathedral Grove

Drive west on BC-4 to start the two-hour trek to Tofino. On your way, you'll pass Cathedral Grove. Vancouver Island and its coastal forests are home to some of the world's tallest Douglas fir trees, about 800 years old and reaching upward of 250 feet into the sky. Cathedral Grove in **Macmillan Provincial Park** is one of the island's most accessible areas of old-growth Douglas firs, and its network of trails meanders underneath the enormous trees.

Tofino

Located in Clayoquot Sound, Tofino is a charming haven of laid-back, seaside spirit where wild meets hip. In the early 1900s, this region was an isolated maritime trading town, accessible only by boat until the logging road was established. Once Tofino was connected to the rest of the land, it quickly drew crowds, and by the 1970s, masses of young people had arrived, establishing the town's iconic surf culture. Respect for nature runs deep here; in the 1990s, it was the epicenter of huge environmental protests called "War in the Woods," with activists and local community members protesting commercial logging interests in Clayoquot Sound. Today Tofino is a very popular tourist destination known for its pristine beaches, great restaurants, incredible accommodations, and locally brewed beer. With remote surf beaches calling to adventurous wave lovers, as well as bald eagles and humpback whales to spot, this is not your average beach town. There's plenty for non-surfers to do as well. See the list below for some ideas.

MORE TO SEE IN TOFINO

Chesterman and Mackenzie Beaches (for tide pools) · Hot Springs Cove, Maquinna Marine Provincial Park · Meares Island · Pacific Rim National Park Reserve · Tonquin Trail · Wild Pacific Trail, Ucluelet

Pacific Rim National Park Reserve is part of the ancestral lands of the Nuu-chah-nulth people.

To return to Washington from Vancouver Island, drive inland back toward Nanaimo. Once you return to Victoria, you can hop back on the Black Ball Ferry Line to continue on your route from Port Angeles.

Hand-carved totem pole along the Nuu-chah-nulth Trail

Off the coast of Tofino

SEQUIM

From Port Angeles, continue your drive for twenty-five minutes east on Highway 101 to Sequim, where you'll pass oodles of lavender fields. Stop at a farm to pick your own bushel. If you're in Sequim between June and August, check the schedule for free outdoor concerts in **Carrie Blake Community Park**. Pack a lunch, or stop by one of Sequim's farm stands for fresh food, and head to **Dungeness Wildlife Refuge**, where you can take a nature walk on the **Dungeness Spit**. The entire hike is 10 miles out to the **New Dungeness Lighthouse** and back; choose whatever distance works for you. Even on a moderately busy day, it doesn't feel too crowded. If you decide to hike all the way out to the lighthouse, check the tide tables first.

PORT TOWNSEND

About thirty minutes east off Highway 101, take WA-20 to Port Townsend, built on the traditional lands of the Klallam. This charming port town flourished through the 1800s, leading to speculation that it might become the largest harbor on the West Coast. While those dreams never came to fruition, in the 1920s, a new paper mill brought economic opportunity. The area prospered during World War II, as soldiers from the three surrounding forts would spend their time in town. **Fort Worden State Park** has an interlacing network of trails through which to walk and discover the old structures. Port Townsend is one of only three Victorian seaports on the National Register of Historic Places. Recent years have seen a boatbuilding industry thrive here, with everything from wooden sailboats to mega yachts being constructed. Visit the **Northwest Maritime Museum** to learn more.

BAINBRIDGE ISLAND

Veer off Highway 101 onto Highway 104, making your way to Bainbridge Island. The Suquamish were the most established people on the island when British explorer George Vancouver arrived in 1792, and by 1855, they had been pushed out. Learn how the area became what it is today at the **Bainbridge Island Historical Museum**. In the early 1900s, Japanese American immigrant families planted the first strawberry farms, leading to the island's agricultural success. During World War II, Bainbridge Island was the first place on the West Coast that forced the Japanese to leave, sending them to internment camps, a dark chapter in the island's history commemorated by the **Bainbridge Island Japanese American Exclusion Memorial**. An easy ferry ride from Seattle, Bainbridge Island is a popular weekend destination for those escaping the city. The **Bainbridge Island Museum of Art** is free and offers rotating exhibits with an emphasis on local artists. There are plenty of food options near the museum, and Winslow Way will take you into the downtown hub. From Bainbridge Island, take WA-305 to the ferry across Elliott Bay into Seattle. Exit your car and go upstairs to the observation deck for a view of the Seattle skyline and the Olympic Mountains.

SEATTLE

In 1851, a group of immigrants from Illinois settled in Seattle and named it after local Native American chief Sealth. The lumber, coal, and shipbuilding industries gave Seattle its robust beginnings until 1889, when a fire devastated the city, which was built of wood. The town was rebuilt literally on top of the old one, and parts of the old city can be accessed today by booking an underground tour. Seattle's progress was hardly halted by the fire; in fact, it inspired improvements to the city's planning and rebuilding with brick and stone. The Boeing factory and later Microsoft and Amazon have contributed to the thriving industry of modern-day Seattle. Surrounded by water and mountain views, Seattle is also privileged to have a beautiful setting. Though the region is known for its gray and rainy days, the climate makes for a lush, verdant landscape, so it's no wonder that Seattle is known as the Emerald City.

Whether you're spending a few hours here or a few days, you shouldn't miss **Pike Place Market**. Look for its iconic signage above the building. Opened in 1907, it is one of the oldest continually operated public farmers' markets in the United States, known for its stands of fresh fish, flowers, and produce. Visit the market's many indoor shops, including **Old Seattle Paperworks**, for vintage ephemera, magazines, and posters. A few blocks south on 1st Avenue is the **Seattle Art Museum**, opened in 1933. Even if you don't have time to explore the museum, you can still get an art fix in the lobby from the Middle Fork installation by John Grade, an enormous sculpture showcasing the silhouette of a 140-year-old western hemlock tree. A few blocks away is the waterfront, where you can take a ride on the **Seattle Great Wheel** for views of the city and Elliott Bay. Make a reservation for dinner at the **Pink Door**, a popular Italian restaurant on the bay that features musical performances, burlesque shows, and trapeze acts.

Near the lively neighborhood of Capitol Hill, **Volunteer Park** is home to both the **Volunteer Park Conservatory**, a haven of plants in a Victorian-style greenhouse, and the **Asian Art Museum**, which exhibits a thorough collection of paintings, pottery, and textiles. From the museum's outdoor garden, you can see Seattle's iconic **Space Needle** in the distance. Bibliophiles will want to visit the **Elliott Bay Book Company** and the **Seattle Public Library**.

North of downtown, cross over the Fremont Bridge to head to the bohemian neighborhood of Fremont, known for its funky vibe. Peruse the antiques at **Fremont Vintage Mall**. Right under the Aurora Bridge, you'll find the famous **Fremont Troll**, a giant concrete sculpture that "watches" over the neighborhood. To the west, the former fishing hub of Ballard still maintains its maritime roots, which you can see firsthand at the **Ballard Locks**, where Puget Sound, Lake Union, and Lake Washington meet. Ships enter the locks and water rises or falls to the level of the destination waterway. Look for migrating salmon mid-June through October, and bask in the surrounding 7 acres of gardens while watching the ships go by.

Our trip ends here. To get home, the Sea-Tac Airport is just 14 miles south on 1-5 from Seattle's city center.

Pike Place Market

MORE TO SEE IN SEATTLE

The architecture (take a Seattle Architecture Foundation walking tour) · Chihuly Garden and Glass · Discovery Park · the Museum of Flight · the Museum of Pop Culture · Olympic Sculpture Park · the view from the Space Needle's observation deck

The Fremont Troll

FRESH
LOCAL
ROCK
FISH
$5.99/lb

FRESH WILD
LOCAL KING
SALMON

Grown in
Washington
Rainier
Cherries
$7.99/lb

Morels
$49.99/LB

ROAD TRIP SCAVENGER HUNT

A little something to occupy your passengers.

VEHICLES

☐ Red convertible

☐ Custom-painted van

☐ Four motorcycles in a row

☐ Volkswagen Beetle

☐ Limousine

☐ Airstream trailer

☐ Tow truck

☐ Dog sticking its head out of a car window

☐ Two dogs in a car

☐ Driver who's eating

☐ School bus

☐ Car with five or more bumper stickers

☐ Florida license plate

☐ Stuffed animals in the rear of a car

☐ Food truck

☐ Logging truck

☐ Pickup truck filled with plants

☐ Car with a "Just Married" sign on it

☐ Car with a surfboard on top

LINING THE ROAD

- ☐ Rainbow flag
- ☐ Surf shop
- ☐ Crab shack
- ☐ Fruit stand
- ☐ Whale mural
- ☐ Skateboarder
- ☐ Jogger
- ☐ Hitchhiker
- ☐ Three bicyclists in a row

- ☐ "Going Out of Business" sign
- ☐ Five sailboats
- ☐ Golf course
- ☐ Cows
- ☐ Elk
- ☐ Clothes on a clothesline
- ☐ Car wash
- ☐ Topiary
- ☐ Person carrying a surfboard

IN THE SKY

- ☐ Kite
- ☐ Flock of seagulls
- ☐ Cloud in the shape of a heart
- ☐ Helicopter
- ☐ Skywriting message

- ☐ Hot-air balloon
- ☐ Plane with a banner
- ☐ Hang glider
- ☐ Crescent moon
- ☐ Rainbow

BEFORE WE PART

Now that this long and winding trip has come to an end, I have one parting wish: that wherever your own journey takes you, you too will discover nature's gifts with a sense of wonderment and reverence. I hope that you will be inspired, not just to explore and enjoy but also to protect. The ocean, the shores, the rocks, the sun, the trees, and the millions of creatures that roam the earth are all connected. We humans have to find our balance within this complex ecosystem that we call home.

ACKNOWLEDGMENTS

Love and gratitude to Mom, Dad, Adam, and Hilary for always supporting me through my creative endeavors.

To my car companions who made my West Coast road trips so memorable: Jenny, Ren, Von, Wade, Ryan, Millie, Mom, Jeremy, and Jamie; thank you for the sunny good times, even when it was raining. A special thanks to my emotional support crew: Jordan, Nic, Connie, Bev, and Jenna.

My deepest thanks to everyone who shared their talents in bringing this book to life: Kate Woodrow, Anna Brones, and Shoshana Gutmajer and the incredible team at Artisan: Lia Ronnen, Jane Treuhaft, Elise Ramsbottom, Sibylle Kazeroid, Nancy Murray, and Raphael Geroni.

Danielle Kroll is an artist and designer known for her paintings and illustrations inspired by travel, nature, and her ever-growing collection of vintage memorabilia. After working as a designer for Anthropologie, she went out on her own to work with clients including Anthropologie, Kate Spade New York, Red Cap Cards, Papyrus, Hallmark, and Figo Fabrics. Kroll lives in upstate New York. Find her on Instagram @daniellekroll.